SPIRIT-BORN CREATIVITY

by

Mark and Patti Virkler

Destiny Image Publishers
P.O. Box 351
Shippensburg, PA 17257

"Speaking to the Purposes of God for this Generation"

ISBN 1-56043-004-4

For Worldwide Distribution
Printed in the U.S.A.

This manual is the result of the united efforts of both authors. The concepts and ideas are a culmination of cooperative study and revelation. The experiences described are common to both. The pronoun "I" is used to demonstrate the unity of our thoughts. This is an expansion of, enlargement and addition to the truths found in **Developing Heart Faith** by the same authors.

TABLE OF CONTENTS

STAGE THREE — BIRTH

APPENDICES

It is recommended that the course **Communion with God** complete with audios or videos by Mark & Patti Virkler be studied and experienced in a group setting before beginning this course. If this cannot be done, please read and apply their book **Dialogue with God**. This will prepare you to receive maximum benefit from this study.

INTRODUCTION

WHO? ME? CREATIVE?!!!

A Quiz on Your Beliefs Concerning Creativity

(Write "true" or "false" in the blank provided.)

_____ 1. To be creative means imagining, or doing something completely new.
_____ 2. Only the experts can create anything meaningful.
_____ 3. Only a gifted minority of people are creative.
_____ 4. Creativity borders on insanity.
_____ 5. If you really have creative ability, someone will discover you and recognize your talents.
_____ 6. Ideas are like magic: you don't have to work for them.
_____ 7. Creative thinking is nice but impractical.
_____ 8. Creativity means complexity.
_____ 9. The best way has already been found.

Hopefully you did not check true for any of these, since each of these statements is false, as has been demonstrated over and over throughout history. (See many such examples in the book **Imagineering** by Michael LeBoeuf.)

We think of Einstein as a great creative genius, which he was, but what most people don't realize is that he spent a good portion of his time working in a Swiss patent office. What a great place to be stimulated by the thinking and creativity of others!

We think of Dale Carnegie as a man who created ideas that have enabled millions of people to live happier, more successful and productive lives. However, Carnegie summarized his creativity this way:

"The ideas I stand for are not mine. I borrowed them from Socrates. I swiped them from Chesterfield. I stole them from Jesus. And I put them in a book. If you don't like their rules, whose would you use?"

Many people have created in fields which they had no expertise in. For example, Eli Whitney, who invented the cotton gin, was a school teacher. Samuel Morse and Robert Fulton, inventors of the telegraph and steamboat, respectively, were both artists. Being a non-expert is often a creative asset because you aren't blinded by traditional ways of viewing the problem.

The motivation to create is much more essential than any natural creative genius which one may possess. For example, during World War II, B.F. Goodrich received three thousand employee suggestions per year, and one third of them were good enough to earn cash awards.

Increasing age is more likely to be a facilitator than a detriment to the creative flow within mankind. George Bernard Shaw won a Nobel Prize when he was nearly seventy. When Thomas Jefferson retired to Monticello, he thought up numerous gadgets and innovations while in his seventies and eighties. Dr. George Washington Carver was still turning out useful ideas for agriculture at eighty. Alexander Graham Bell perfected the telephone at fifty-eight and solved the problem of stabilizing the balance in airplanes while in his seventies. Mark Twain wrote two books, **Eve's Dairy** and **The $30,000 Bequest**, at seventy-one. Benjamin Franklin produced one of his greatest works of writing at eighty-four. The list of examples is endless.

Professor Harvey Lehman in a study of approximately one thousand creative achievements listed the median age of the creators at 74 when creativity occurred. All indications are that the more we use our creative abilities, the better they become.

Spirit-born creativity is no accident; it requires purposeful activity. This study manual will open the doors of your understanding, so that the creativity of God can flow through you continuously in ways of which you may have only dreamed. Once you are in flow with the Spirit of God, your only limits lie within God Himself. You will discover yourself doing and being more than you had ever dreamed possible, because you are no longer limited to your abilities. You have now learned to flow in the abilities of Almighty God.

In Chapter One we will discover that creativity is a by-product of intimacy. In Chapter Two we will learn that God has made man creative. In Chapter Three we will see that this creativity is released most fully when we allow God to fill all five senses of our spirit with Himself. In Chapter Four we will see how we need to quiet ourselves so that we can become sensitive to the divine flow. In the next five chapters we will examine step by step how God progressively fills each of the five senses of our spirit with Himself. In Chapter Ten we will discover the principle of death of a vision, and we will learn of the need to take our hands off the vision and move only as God directs us. Chapter Eleven will bring us the conclusion, the fulfillment, which is the birthing of the supernatural creativity of God within us.

Concerning Journaling

This manual requires you to do extensive journaling[1] as you go through it. I would like to mention several things in light of this that may be helpful. 1) Feel free to **revise the questions** so they more perfectly suit your needs. 2) You may struggle finding it difficult to journal about certain **things which you may consider secular**, such as a financial goal or a business project. If so, we must remind ourselves that there are no secular things. All of life is sacred.

For example, when I began working with stock market investment strategies, I was hesitant to journal about it for several reasons. I needed first of all to be sure that God approved of it and that it wasn't gambling. So I journaled about that. Then I was afraid to trust my journaling when it came to such technical things as charting and graphing stocks and choosing which one to invest in. The Lord told me I would not make any money for the first several months, and that I was only to chart until June 1. I couldn't believe I wouldn't make any money, and I wasn't sure about using journaling in such a technical way anyway, so I began to trade commodities doing that which I thought was best.

After making decisions on my own for 3 months and losing on every investment except one small gain, the Lord finally spoke to me in my journal and said, "Mark, could you have done any worse by trusting your journal?" I said, "no" and decided to trust my journal for my next investment. And sure enough, all my previous loses were recouped in just four weeks.

Therefore, a third problem you may have with the journaling assignments in this manual, is that you may feel uncomfortable**trusting** what the Lord says in your journal as you enter new areas with your journaling. That's okay. Accept it as natural. If you need too, skip what God says in your journal

1 The writing out of your prayers and God's answers.

and do it the way you think is best. Then record your results. The next time if you can, follow your journaling and record your results. Allow the **results** to convince you as time goes on. I accept these times as learning times, being hesitant and exploratory is a natural and perfectly acceptable part of life.

For me, developing heart faith and releasing Spirit-born creativity are one and the same. It is as God fills the five senses of my spirit with Himself that heart faith is developed and divine creativity is released. Come now and join us in learning the principles of releasing the creativity of Almighty God.

To Maurice Fuller, Roger Miller,
Mart Vahi and John Watson,
our loyal friends
and spiritual advisors.

Chapter 1

Creativity — A By-Product of Intimacy

Is increasing your personal creativity one of the goals in your life? Do you long to find creative solutions to the problems and situations that face you every day in your home and at work? Do you want to give the world something of lasting beauty? Do you want to improve the quality of life of those around you through inventions and new ideas? Of course you do! Why else would you be reading a book about creativity?

Unfortunately, if you view creativity as a goal toward which you can work, you are already heading in the wrong direction. Creativity, particularly Spirit-born creativity, is not an end in itself. Instead, it is a by-product of a relationship with the Creator of the universe. Creativity is born from the union of the human heart and the Divine heart. It is one of the fruits of intimacy with the Holy Spirit. It grows as one learns to hear his own heart, and the voice of the Holy Spirit within his heart. It increases as one learns to hear the hearts of others, and blend that which is being heard into new creations.

In my early years as a Christian, I knew very little about creativity. And it is no wonder, since I knew nothing of how to have fellowship with the Holy Spirit. I didn't know how to contact Him, or what His stirrings within me felt like. I couldn't hear the voice of God or dialogue with Him as men and women did throughout the Scriptures. My Christianity was a theology, a creed, and a doctrine, rather than a day by day living experience. No wonder I couldn't release the creativity of Almighty God! I know I was saved, because my heart was toward God, and I was doing all I knew to experience Him. It was just that my knowledge of how to experience a God who is Spirit was extremely limited. The rationalism of the age had crept into my church, and thus all they could offer me was a Gospel creed, not a super-rational encounter with the God of the Bible. Furthermore, I was untrained and unskilled in hearing the hearts of others.

Establishing Intimacy with God

It took me ten years of wandering as a Christian, followed by one year of intensive searching, to finally break through to the other side of silence and discover intimacy with the One who lived within me. When I finally learned how, it wasn't hard at all. Why, a child could easily do it! Remember that Jesus said, "Suffer the little children to come unto me for of such is the Kingdom of heaven." When my daughter was eight years old, she learned to hear the voice of the Creator within her heart. And like all who do so, she found more than simply a voice. We found a person who heals us and loves us much more deeply than we could have ever dreamed. No wonder Paul called it an incomprehensible love.

What I have to say in this book on releasing the creativity of Almighty God is based on the assumption that one can experience the voice of the Holy Spirit within his heart, and has learned to live out of His wonderful healing power. If you are still caught in the web of rational Christianity and are trying to break free, I recommend you set this book aside for a few months, and instead study my earlier book Communion With God, which tells in detail the steps God took me through in learning to hear His voice. It is a teaching manual, designed to be studied in a small group setting, or at least with one other friend. It is important that you have someone to be a sounding board as you experience this new way of living.

Anyone can follow the steps laid out in *Communion with God.* They are not hard. We even have an edition for teen-agers. If you will follow the guidelines within it, you will break through into intimacy with the God of this universe. My life has not been the same since I learned to dialogue with God and clearly hear His voice. Your life can be affected the same way.

In *Communion With God*, we teach you how to quiet yourself and tune to God's voice (which often comes as a flow of spontaneous thoughts), use vision, and begin writing down the spontaneous healing, life-giving flow that comes from deep within your heart and spirit. This is the river of life that the Bible says will flow out of your innermost being (Jn. 7:37-39). It is the Holy Spirit Whom all who believed were to receive. This is real Christianity. It is power and life! It is God Himself!

When you are living in regular, consistent communion with God, you will be on the road to the release of Spirit-Born Creativity.

Establishing Intimacy with Your Own Heart

For me, however, Spirit-born creativity was not the next step. Instead, I needed to be healed emotionally by the voice and vision of Almighty God. He began to speak love and healing into my heart that eradicated years of built up hurts and sins. Only His voice could take away those blockages that had accumulated through the years. Yes, His blood had already justified me in God's sight, but I still lived in the midst of many struggles. Divine perspective, healing, understanding and release from these struggles have come through hearing His voice. My book *Counseled By God* tells how God's voice can and does heal anger, guilt, condemnation, depression, inferiority and accusation while releasing the Christian into faith, hope, love, identity in Christ and much more.

Somewhere in this travelogue everyone must learn to abide in Christ. For me, that meant not doing things myself, but being conscious of, and reliant upon, the One who stands beside me, lives within me and surrounds me. Christ-consciousness needed to replace self-consciousness. Therefore, I spent a year learning to "abide in Christ" and, of course, wrote a study manual about it.

Now, why do I tell you all this? Is it to sell you my books or tell you how great I am? No! I am firmly convinced that each of us must learn similar lessons in our walk with God. It is a walk, one step at a time. If you try to jump over steps, it just turns into a mess. It you try to rush steps, it becomes an academically oriented Christian theology, and profits little. It took me a year to learn each of the above three lessons. I spent one year learning to commune with God, one year learning to abide in Christ, and one year allowing God to heal the hurts and sin bondages within my life. Then God saw fit to teach me Spirit born creativity. And I have taken a year to learn this also.

Discern Where You Are on Your Spiritual Pilgrimage

Therefore I recommend that you prayerfully decide where you are in your walk with God, and what God wants to be your next step. If this book is it, then go for it! If it is some other life lesson, then by all means set this one down and pick up the appropriate one. We are talking about a life here. Yours! Give it what it needs. Give it what God is instructing you to give.

Do not seek creativity as a gift in itself, something devoid of a relationship with the Creative One. Instead, recognize it as the outflow of a full and complete life. If you seek to shortcut the road and take the "easy" way, you may find someone lurking in the shadows awaiting you. He awaited Jesus, and offered Him a shortcut to getting the nations to bow down and worship Him. However, Jesus refused to accept it. He took the road of intimacy with the Father, saying, "I do nothing on my own initiative...." We must be those who also say, "I do nothing on my own initiative." Therefore, be sure that you establish intimacy with the Creator first so that your creativity flows as a by-product of the Creative One, and you are not tempted to worship at the shrine of Christian humanism.

Man's Own Creativity

You see, man's heart is creative because we are made after the image of God. Therefore, man can release the creativity of his own heart and become conceited, seeing how great it is. Then he falls into a snare set by the trapper. This is what the New Age movement has done. They have discovered the creativity of man's heart and are learning how to release it. However, they do not recognize the Divine Creator, and therefore fall into the sin of worshipping man. Therefore, shortcuts are not always shortcuts. Often they are "longcuts."

Establishing Intimacy with Others

The other thing I want to encourage you in as you begin this study, is to recognize the value of interpersonal relationships in the release of creativity. God has made mankind to live and operate within a social setting. No man can exist if he lives alone. It takes at least two (a man and a woman) simply to continue to propagate the race. God says that one can put

1000 to flight and two, 10,000. Man's creativity is greatly multiplied as he teams up and learns and grows together with others. Probably the more open his heart and mind are to others, the faster he will grow and the more creative he will become. I grew up in a church that believed they were the only ones going to heaven. Not much chance for creativity or cross pollination there. And the fruit was evident. I consider that church to be at least 50 years out of touch with reality.

Today, I am open to learn from almost anyone. I read and study thousands of books from many different traditions. Not that I agree with all that is said, but I find much truth and insight in those whom I would consider absolute heathen. God does rain on both the just and the unjust.

You may say, "But aren't you in danger of being deceived if you receive so widely for so many?" Not really, because I have a safeguard in submission to effective spiritual covering. When I feel I may be getting out on a limb, I check with them and see if they can cover me. If they can't, I back down.

Therefore I encourage you to expand your heart to receive from many around. Listen to them. Hear their hearts. Let them teach you. Let them cross pollinate you and you will become much more creative than ever before. I promise you that the greatest lessons I have learned and steps of growth I have taken in my life have come when I have stepped outside my immediate church culture and received insight from those who were very different from me. So embrace your fears. Establish a solid spiritual shepherd, and reach out beyond yourself to discover new horizons. You will not be disappointed. You will enter a whole new world of creativity. Blessings as you travel!

Chapter 2

God Has Made Man Creative

God, the Creator of the universe, has "made man after His own image," a powerful phrase, especially in the Hebrew text. [1] God breathed into man the breath of life, and man became a living soul.

The Humanist — Drawing from the Creativity within Man's Own Spirit

Because of the breath of God that has been placed within man, man now finds himself creative and capable of fantastic feats. Some men discover this fabulous creativity which God has placed within them and decide to use it to the fullest. This we call humanism. This man has learned to move from his head to his heart, where the creative breath of God still functions, and draw forth from this creativity. However, for the humanist, the creativity of God is never fully realized.

The Spirit-filled Christian — Drawing from the Creativity of God within Man's Spirit

Even though God created man like Himself, (i.e., a little

1 The phrase "image of God" in the Old Testament literally means "little gods."

god, according to the Hebrew of the Old Testament)*, God never intended that man operate as an autonomous individual. Man was always to be part of something larger than himself. He was to be a branch grafted into a Vine, a temple that contained Another. He was to allow the life of the God who made him to flow through him. In this way he would release the full creativity of God into the world in which he lived. He was not to use his creativity himself, but rather, he was to yield it to Almighty God. Man is commanded to "be filled with the Spirit of God" and "to walk in the Spirit." Man is to be **found "in Christ," not "in himself."**

The creativity of a man with this **dependent posture**, will be far greater than the creativity released by the man who only looks to the creativity of his own spirit. Not only will the dependent man release the creativity of his God-given spirit; he will go far beyond this, releasing the creativity of God the Creator of the universe, as He looks to God and tunes to the spontaneity of the Holy Spirit flow.

The Rationalist — the Non-creative One

The man who will be least creative will the man who has not yet discovered how to live out of the spontaneous bubble of the spirit world, the man who still walks through life living only out of the reasonings of his mind.

The Cultist — the One Who Creates in the Negative

The worst of all eventualities is for satan to fill the creative capacities of man. In this case, the creativity of man's spirit is being used in reverse. Man is poising his heart before an evil thought or an evil vision. Man is incubating it, and thus releasing the destructive power of satan into the world in which he lives. These basic approaches are diagrammed on page 9.

Four Possible Stances

Approach # 1 - Holy Spirit-filled living

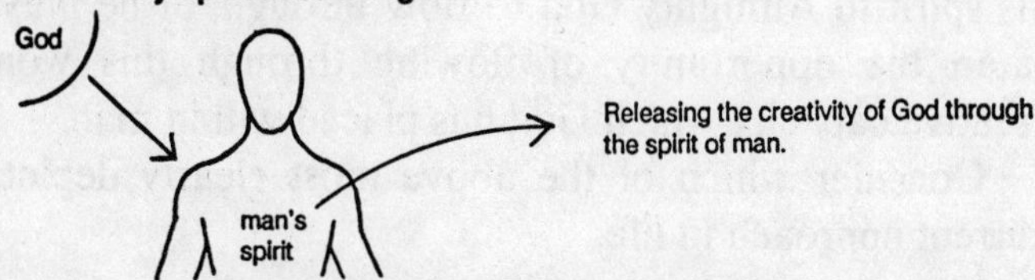

This is the typical stance of a born-again Christian who has learned to walk in the Spirit, that is, learned to live out of the bubbling of the Holy Spirit (river of life) within him.

Approach # 2 - Releasing the power of satan

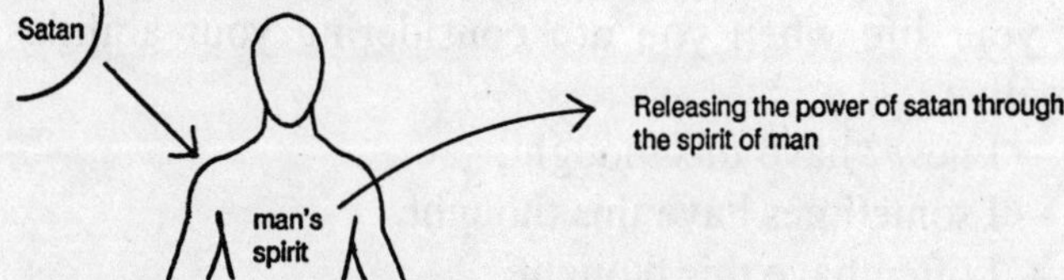

This is the typical stance of a person involved in cultism, anger, bitterness, wrath, dissension, accusation, condemnation, destruction, etc.

Approach #3 - Humanism - releasing man's own creativity

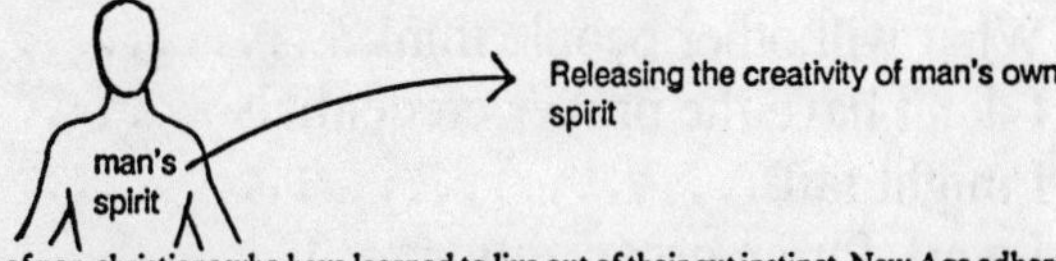

Typical stance of non-christians who have learned to live out of their gut instinct, New Age adherents, who have discovered the creativity that resides within the heart of man, and Christians who live only on the level releasing the greatness of man.

Approach #4 - Rationalism - releasing the power of the mind

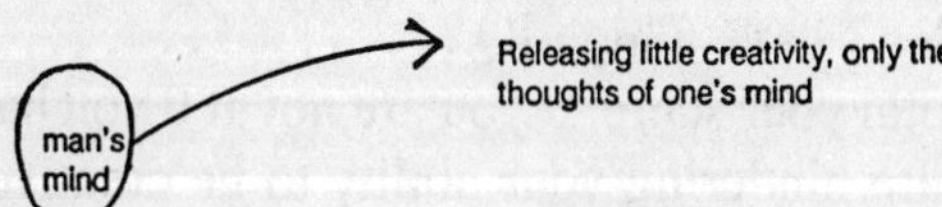

Typical of non-Christians who have not learned to relax and go with the flow, and Christians who have not learned yet to live out of the voice of God, but rather, they live out of laws, principles, and boxes which they have discovered.

So we see that man is very creative. He may choose to use his creativity himself. He may choose to yield the capacities of his spirit to Almighty God to flow through, or he may allow satan the opportunity of flowing through this wonderful creative capacity which God has placed within man.

Consider which of the above most clearly depicts your current approach in life.

Ideas One May Hold that Hinder One's Ability to be Creative

Circle the number that best represents the current experience of your life when you are considering your abilities to be creative

0 — I never have this thought,
1 — I sometimes have this thought,
2 — I often have this thought.

1. I'm too old.	0	1	2
2. I'm too busy.	0	1	2
3. What will other people think?	0	1	2
4. I don't have the proper credentials	0	1	2
5. I might fail!	0	1	2
6. I work for an organization; I can't be creative.	0	1	2
7. I'm a woman; men are the ingenious ones.	0	1	2
8. I don't have a high IQ	0	1	2

Total your score. If you are not at 0 you have some attitudes that are hindering your ability to be creative. Seek to change these attitudes to some that are more productive for effective living.

You may want to memorize Philippians 4:8 as an antidote:

"I can do all things through Christ who strengthens me"

More Killer Phrases that Stop the Flow of Creative Ideas

It won't work...
It won't pan out...
Here we go again...
Too old-fashioned...
We're too big for that...
It'll mean more work...
That's not our problem...
We're not ready for it yet...
It's not our responsibility...
They'll think we are weird...
We have too many projects now...
We've never done it that way before...
Let's discuss it at some other time...
You don't understand the problem...
Sounds good but I don't think it will work...
We've never used that approach before...
We have always done it that way so it must be good...
Let's think it over for a while and watch developments...
It's all right in theory, but can you put it into practice...
Yes, but...
It's not tradition...
It's not in the plan...
We're too small for that...
We haven't the time...
Don't move too fast...

Seek to steer clear of these ideas in yourself and others. They destroy your ability to be creative.

A Wide-angle View of How the Creative Capacity Works

Step One involves **insight**. You see a problem, a need or a solution to a problem, and you decide to go to work on it.

Step Two involves **preparation**. You prepare yourself to birth a creative solution by using all your senses and thoroughly investigating and exploring possible ways in which the idea can be developed and expanded. As you go to the Lord for direction, you may find that He does not want you to explore all possible ways, but He may direct you on a certain path of exploration. This divine direction can save you countless hours of hard work.

Step Three involves **incubation**. You turn the problem over to your heart, your subconscious mind, your right brain, and let it ponder it. Take a walk, a nap, a bath, sleep on it for a weekend, or whatever. Find a way to relax. Present the issue in a relaxed manner before the Lord, and allow Him to gently mold and sift it until it clicks and forms a perfect picture.

Step Four involves **verification**. Using intelligent judgment and experimentation from Scripture, you test the inspirations and decide whether they are confirmed or denied. Let the peace of God rule in your heart. Let others test it, also. Obviously it can and will be tested by its fruit. As you work through the testing process, revise the ideas as necessary.

The five senses of your spirit which we will speak of in the next chapter are used in Steps Two and Three, especially. In Step Two, the voice and vision of God is used to guide you in knowing what you are to research and investigate, and you use them to guide you in the ongoing process of investigation. In Step Three, you are pondering deep within your heart as you become involved in the incubation process.

Personal Application

In closing this chapter on learning to recognize God's gift of creativity to man, let's do one more self check on the four steps we have discussed. Circle the appropriate number.

I do this: 1. rarely 2. sometimes 3. often.

Insight: I see a problem, need, or solution. ..	1	2	3
Preparation: I use all my senses, combined with prayer, in the exploratory process. ...	1	2	3

Incubation: I relax so my heart can work
on it. 1 2 3
Verification: I expose these creative ideas
to ruthless verification. 1 2 3

If your score is high, rejoice. If it is not high, rejoice, anyway, because in this course you are going to learn, with God's help, how to become comfortable living this process.

Chapter 3

Overview of the Five Senses of Man's Spirit and How God Desires to Fill Them

Heart faith: one of the most treasured possessions of all times. The gift given by God, which, when incubated within, brings forth the purposes of God. The faith that moves mountains, heals the sick, and generates glorious supernatural provision.

How is it found? How is it grown? Is it found in the Bible? Is it found in a creed or technique? Is it found in righteous living? Precisely speaking, it is not found in any of the above. It is found in God alone. Head belief can begin with man, but heart faith always beings with God. God speaks revelation into your heart, and then grants you an accompanying vision, as he did with Abraham, "the Father of Faith." First, God spoke the promise to Abraham. Then, He gave him a vision of the promise fulfilled by showing him the stars of heaven and the sands of the seashore. Thus Abraham began incubating the voice and vision of God, allowing the other three senses of the spirit to become totally consumed with them. Abraham filled the mind of his spirit with the word from the Lord. He committed his inner will to speak only the promise and vision of God. The emotions of his spirit became so charged with the voice and vision of God that they moved him to act in faith upon the promises of God. In due time, God brought forth both the death of the vision and then the supernatural fulfillment of it.

Thus we have it, the way heart faith is received, incubated, and finally delivered forth as a supernatural miracle.

We shall in this manual more closely examine each of these six stages from inception to fulfillment, examining the five senses of man's heart or spirit, and how God fills all five in the development of heart faith. As Dr. Paul Yonggi Cho describes it, one becomes pregnant with the dream and rhema of God.

The pattern of our study: (Please examine these verses.)

ABRAHAM — THE FATHER OF FAITH

1. **Heard** the Voice of the Lord — Gen. 12:1-3 2. **Saw** With Eyes of Faith — Gen. 15:5,6	**Conception**
3. **Thought** With a Heart of Faith — Rom. 4:20,21 4. **Spoke** the Word of Faith — Gen. 17:5 5. **Acted** in Faith — Gen. 17:23	**Incubation**
6. Experienced Death of the Vision — Gen. 17:18,19 7. Received the Promise of Faith — **Gen. 21:5**	**Birth**

The graph on page 18 demonstrates the five senses of man's spirit and how God desires to fill them.

Throughout this text we will carefully examine each aspect of this diagram. We will spend a chapter on each of the five senses of man's spirit and how they can be filled with God, satan, or man. We will teach you how to be aware of these five senses of your spirit throughout the day. You will be able to instantly discern who is filling them, and what stage of the process you are in at any given moment, concerning any given issue. This will allow you to flow cooperatively with God at all times, birthing His life in the midst of every situation.

The process of filling these five senses is really quite simple and automatic. We do it unconsciously all day long.

Essentially, you begin by getting an idea. Then you get a picture of its fulfillment. Next you take some time and ponder it. Then you decide to speak it forth, and finally, you act on it, birthing through the creative capacities of your spirit that which has been conceived and incubated within it.

Incubating Only Christ

	SENSE	HOW USED	BIBLE EXAMPLE	STAGE
1.	Inner Ear (Jn 5:30)	Receives God's Rhema	Gen 12:1-3	CONCEPTION
2.	Inner Eye (Rev 4:1)	Receives God's Vision	Gen 15:5,6	
3.	Inner Mind (Lk 2:19)	Ponders God's Thoughts	Rom 4:20,21	INCUBATION
4	Inner Will (Acts 19:21)	Speaks on God's Rhema	Gen 17:5	
5.	Inner Emotions (1 Kings 21:5)	Acts on God's Rhema And Vision	Gen 17:23	
	END RESULT	Death of the Vision "I" am unable to Bring it about	Gen 16:2 Gen 17:18,19	BIRTH
		Supernatural resurrection of the Vision. "In the fullness of Time GOD brings it forth."	Gen 21:1,2 Gal 4:4a	

Fixing our eyes on Jesus, the author and perfector of our faith" Heb. 12:2
"I am the Alpha and the Omega, the first and the Last, the begining and the end." Rev. 22:13

Birthing Life or Death Through our Spirits is Continuous and Automatic

Let's consider a common example of birthing both life and death through the creative capacities of your spirit.
Situation: You are offered a new ministry opportunity or job advancement, in which you have had absolutely no experience.

Creating Death By Filling All Five Senses of Your Spirit With Satan

1. You get an **idea** that you could never do that.
2. You get a **picture** of yourself failing.
3. You begin to **ponder** these thoughts and pictures.
4. You begin to **speak** them forth.
5. You **act,** turning down the opportunity.

Creating Life By Filling All Five Senses of Your Spirit With God

1. As you pray about the situation, **God speaks** that He is going before you, and will grant you all gifts necessary for effectiveness and success in this new venture.
2. **God gives you a vision** of His life effectively flowing through you as you step into this new venture.
3. You **ponder** these thoughts and pictures.
4. You begin to **speak** them forth.
5. You **act**, stepping boldly forth to embrace this new opportunity.

A Brief Scriptural Review of Faith

1. Faith defined:

"Faith is the substance (firm conviction) of things hoped for, the evidence of things not seen (Heb. 11:1)."
"That which is seen was not made out of things which are visible (Heb. 11:3)."

2. Faith's Inception:

"Faith comes by hearing and hearing by the word (rhema) of Christ (Rom.10:17)."

3. Faith's Necessity:

"Without faith it is impossible to please Him, for he who comes to God must believe that He is and that He is a rewarder of those who seek Him (Heb. 11:6)."

"Whatever is not of faith is sin (Rom. 14:23)."

4. Faith Illustrated:

Abraham — "the father of all who believe (Rom. 4:11)"

"Who follow in the steps of the faith of our father, Abraham (Rom. 4:12)"

"...Abraham who is the father of us all (Rom. 4:16)"

Abraham — "grew strong in faith (Rom. 4:20)"

Personal Application

Become aware of this automatic experience of filling the five senses of your heart by taking a **situation, issue,** or **thought** which you have encountered over the last several days, and jot down how you have progressively filled the five senses of your spirit as you have worked with it. Record your responses below. If possible choose a "positive" experience so that you will be edified. However, even a "negative" one will be a learning experience for you.

The situation, issue or thought was...

1. The thought which I chose to receive concerning it was...

2. The picture or vision which I chose to connect to it was...

3. I began to ponder this thought, thinking... (also discuss how you pondered it)

4. I began to speak it forth in this way...

5. I began to act it out in this way...

6. I observed its birthing in the following manner...

Now take another issue or situation which you are currently facing and go through the same steps, this time carefully journaling through steps 1 through 5. Notice the tremendous life and creativity that is birthed when this process is bathed in journaling.

The situation, issue, or thought was...

1. "Lord, what do you want to speak to me concerning this situation?"

2. "Lord, let me see this situation as you see it."

3. Ponder the voice and vision of Almighty God.

4. Ask God how He wants you to speak it forth. Record what He says and begin speaking as He asks you to.

5. Ask God if there is any specific action He wants you to take. Record it and begin acting as God directs.

6. Record what God births through you.

Concluding Prayer: Thank you, Lord, for making me more aware of this ongoing process of creating through my spirit.

Chapter 4

Preparation for Receiving God's Creative Ideas

"Be still and know... (Ps. 46:10)"
"My soul waits in silence for God only, for my hope is in Him (Ps. 62:5)."

Nothing will release the creativity of man's spirit, or the Holy Spirit within man's spirit, more than inwardly quieting the mind and the heart before God. Just as internal pressure cuts off the creative flow, internal peace releases it.

"My peace I give unto thee...," says our Lord. As Christians we must learn to capture this peace and abide in it. Through it we shall obtain maximum opportunity to release God's creative flow through our hearts. Without it we shall avail little.

God has designed man to operate at peak efficiency when abiding in His peace. When relaxed, the capillaries on the right side of the brain open up allowing more blood to this portion of your being. The intuitive flow comes through the right side of your brain. Peace is a fruit of His Holy Spirit which is grown as we abide and commune with Him. God also fills us with faith, hope, and love, and He commands us to dwell on those things which are lovely, just, pure, peaceable, of good report, etc. When we are living in these positives, we are operating at peak performance, our Creator is glorified, and His creativity is most able to flow freely through us.

So above all, we must learn to live in the peace of God which surpasses all understanding. The inner obstacles which have the greatest tendency to block this inner pose of peace are anger, guilt, fear, and insecurity. Each of these obstacles is dealt with in depth in the text **Counseled by God** by the same author, so we will not deal extensively with how they are healed at this time. We refer the interested reader to this text.

One thing I will say at this time, however, is that for me, this inner peace was only achieved as I learned to commune with God. I will go to God with my inner frustrations, and express them to Him, and He will begin to speak to me concerning them. He will tell me how He sees the situation, how He wants me to respond to the situation, and to believe in His power over it, being patient while He works it out. I find that after receiving and recording these words, and correcting my thoughts and heart according to His instruction, peace will again flow, and along with it, God's creativity.

Therefore, I cannot emphasize enough the importance of learning to commune with God, and then *doing it.* I have written two books of instruction concerning this. One is entitled **Communion With God**, and the other, **Dialogue With God**. Both or either are recommended for the one seeking to learn this skill. I will briefly discuss how one receives the voice and vision of God in the next two chapters. We also have available **A Journal**, in which you can record your dialogue with God. All of these texts may be ordered from the order sheet in the back of this manual.

Some General Strategies for Achieving Peace of Mind

1. Pray to see how God wants you to handle the situation that is distracting you from an attitude of peace. Ask Him what He wants you to do about it. Write down both your question and His answer on a sheet of paper. As His voice often comes as a flow of spontaneous ideas, tune to spontaneity. See Him present with you as you pray; He **is** present with you.
2. Make a conscious attempt to walk in the Lord's presence every minute. Read **Practicing the Presence of God**, by Brother Lawrence, for additional help in this area. Practice seeing Jesus present with you. Quietly worship and commune with Him throughout the day.
3. Spend time quietly before the Lord's presence, receiving from Him. Be responsive to His ideas.
4. Remember that "a merry heart doeth good like medicine." Keep laughing. Don't take yourself too seriously. Work in a spirit of playfulness.
5. Focus on one thing at a time.
6. Use personal touches that relax you.
7. Think visually. (This involves using the right side of your brain, which is also where the intuitive process stems from.) Be responsive to this intuitive flow.
8. Make it a point to give your life away to others, because in losing your life, you find it.

Four Emotions that Disrupt Peace of Mind

There are four commonly experienced emotions in life that disrupt one's peace of mind. They are anger, guilt, fear and insecurity. There is nothing wrong with sensing these emotions. However it is important that we process them quickly and effectively in the Lord's presence so we can go on experiencing a creative life.

Are you processing these emotions quickly and effectively and returning to the creative flow or do you get stuck living in one or several of these emotions? To allow you to hear from God concerning these issues please complete the following journaling exercise.

Personal Application (Note to instructor: some of this may be completed in class.)

To help you arrive at inner peace, you may wish to record God's answers to you concerning some of the following questions.

Lord, what would you like to speak to me concerning the way I process my anger?

Lord, what would you like to speak to me concerning the way I handle guilt?

Lord, what would you like to speak to me concerning the way I handle fear?

Lord, what would you like to speak to me concerning the way I handle feelings of insecurity?

Biblical Meditation — the State of Relaxed Focus

The Bible uses the word meditation to describe being properly poised to receive from God. One who is meditating is relaxed, calm, dependent upon the Holy Spirit, and focused upon God. This is the state into which you will want to enter and live, so that the creative flow of God within you can be continual.

Identifying the Five Key Elements in Meditation

This section will help you look at the five key ingredients of the contemplative or meditative state and will help you determine how present these are in your life.

Meditation is characterized by physical calm, focused attention, letting be, receptivity, and spontaneous flow. The opposites of these characteristics are physical tension, distraction, overcontrol, activity, and analytical thought. These can be placed on a continuum. On each continuum, place an "X" at the point which you feel characterizes your overall life.

Physical Tension — Physical Calm

0 1 2 3 4 5

Distraction — Focused Attention

0 1 2 3 4 5

Overcontrol — Letting Be

0 1 2 3 4 5

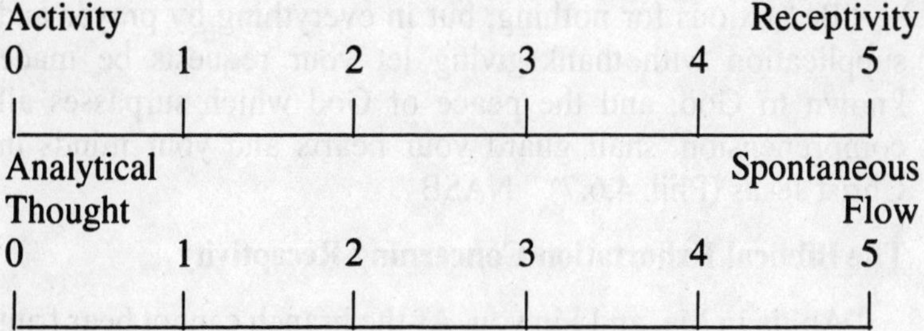

Meditation is commanded throughout the Scriptures, and so are each of these elements that make up the meditative pose. Consider the following with me.

The Biblical Exhortation Concerning Physical Calm

"There remains therefore a Sabbath rest for the people of God. For the one who has entered His rest has himself also rested from his works, as God did from His. Let us therefore be diligent to enter that rest, lest anyone fall through following the same example of disobedience (Heb. 4:9-11)."

"And to whom did He swear that they should not enter His rest, but to those who were disobedient? And so we see that they were not able to enter because of unbelief (Heb. 3:18,19)."

The Biblical Exhortation Concerning Focused Attention

"...Let us...lay aside every encumbrance, and...sin which so easily entangles us and let us run...fixing our eyes on Jesus the author and perfecter of faith... (Heb. 12:1,2)."

"...Truly, truly, I say to you, the Son can do nothing of Himself, unless it is something He sees the Father doing; for whatever the Father does, these things the Son also does in like manner (Jn. 5:19)."

The Biblical Exhortation Concerning Letting Be

"Cease striving (marginal reference: let go, relax) and know that I am God (Ps. 46:10 NASB)."

"Be anxious for nothing, but in everything by prayer and supplication with thanksgiving let your requests be made known to God, and the peace of God which surpasses all comprehension, shall guard your hearts and your minds in Christ Jesus (Phil. 4:6,7)." NASB

The Biblical Exhortation Concerning Receptivity

"Abide in Me, and I in you. As the branch cannot bear fruit of itself, unless it abides in the vine, so neither can you, unless you abide in Me. I am the vine, you are the branches; he who abides in Me, and I in him, he bears much fruit; for apart from Me you can do nothing (Jn. 15:4,5)."

The Biblical Exhortation Concerning Spontaneous Flow

"He who believes in Me, as the Scripture said, 'From his innermost being shall flow rivers of living water.' But this He spoke of the Spirit, whom those who believed in Him were to receive... (Jn. 7:38,39)."

On the following lists check those characteristics which represent your meditative state as well as your general life-style, since meditating or abiding is to be a way of living.

PHYSICAL CALM

____ My heart beats calmly and evenly.
____ My breathing feels calm, easy, even, and complete.
____ My muscles don't feel tense, tight, or clenched up.
____ I don't feel restless and fidgety.
____ I don't feel tense or self-conscious when I say or do something.
____ I don't feel tense, hot, and perspiring.
____ I don't feel the need to go to the bathroom when I don't have to.
____ I feel coordinated.

____ My mouth isn't dry.
____ I feel awake and refreshed.
____ I don't have a headache.
____ I don't have a backache.
____ I don't feel unfit or heavy.
____ My shoulders, neck or back are not tense.
____ The condition of my skin is healthy.
____ My eyes are not watery or teary.
____ My stomach feels calm.
____ My appetite is okay.

FOCUSED ATTENTION

____ My mind is not scattered.
____ I have little trouble remembering what I am doing.
____ I feel very conscious of things.
____ When disrupted, I find it easy to get back on track.
____ My mind feels clear.
____ I feel centered.
____ I am not indecisive.
____ My goals and priorities are clear.
____ I keep things simple, doing one thing at a time.
____ My mind is steady and focused.
____ I concentrate on what I am doing.
____ I seem to be quite perceptive.
____ My mind is not confused.
____ I don't let interruptions disturb me.
____ I keep my mind on what I want to do.
____ Even if things get hectic, I feel I can work in a calm and orderly manner.
____ I feel quite alert.
____ I devote my full attention to what I decide to do.
____ I feel absorbed.
____ My attention doesn't wander.
____ Things seem lucid and clear.

____ It is fairly easy to keep my mind on my task.
____ I don't feel divided between different courses of action.
____ I seem quite aware of things.
____ I don't wander from what I set out to do.
____ I finish one job before starting something else.
____ I live in the present, fully experiencing every moment.
____ My mind is like a mirror, clearly reflecting the physical and spiritual worlds without distortion.

LETTING BE

____ My wants and desires do not drive me.
____ I am not hard on myself, even though I have some imperfections.
____ I don't feel as though I have to urgently push or rush myself.
____ I can accept things that can't be done or understood.
____ It feels okay to say "live and let live" about some of my problems.
____ I can put things that really matter in perspective.
____ I don't get worked up over things that can't be changed.
____ I feel I can let go and be myself.
____ I feel flexible.
____ Some of my wishes seem less important when seen side by side with things that really matter.
____ When I have worked enough, I can easily let go and relax.
____ I feel patient.
____ It feels okay not to worry needlessly about yesterday's or tomorrow's problems.
____ It feels okay to let some things be.
____ I feel as though I can accept my problems philosophically.
____ I don't feel as though everything has to be done at once.

____ I feel things aren't so bad, even when they don't go the way I want.

____ I don't get caught up demanding things I cannot have or that don't really matter.

____ I don't feel particularly self-conscious or as though I have to be overly concerned with doing the right thing or making a good impression.

____ I don't feel as though I have to have everyone's acceptance and approval.

____ I feel part of a larger purpose or scheme of things.

RECEPTIVITY

____ I am aware of God flowing through me.

____ I live in an ongoing dependence upon the Holy Spirit.

____ I acknowledge the Holy Spirit's presence.

____ I do not tackle projects with a dependence upon my own abilities.

____ I offer one word or sentence prayers when in need.

____ I am instantly aware when pride or self-dependence encroaches upon me.

____ I picture myself as one filled with Another.

____ I recognize that my strength comes from God.

____ I recognize that my wisdom comes from God.

____ I recognize that God is my source.

____ I picture myself as one through whom Another flows.

____ I am aware that I can do nothing on my own.

____ I am aware that my righteousness is that which is imputed through Christ.

____ I see myself as clothed with Christ's righteousness.

____ I picture myself as a container filled with Another.

____ When I succeed, I am immediately aware that it is Christ's victory.

____ When I fail, I am aware that I have not drawn on the One Who lives within.

____ I do things without undue strain or effort.

SPONTANEOUS FLOW

____ I live tuned to spontaneity.
____ I recognize the Holy Spirit's flow as an inner flow from deep within (John 7:37-39).
____ I am willing to, and comfortable about living **in flow**.
____ I feel uncomfortable living in boxes.
____ I feel that pure analysis is not as profitable as allowing spontaneity to flow together with analysis.
____ I am comfortable going with inner promptings.
____ I feel spontaneous and free.
____ I feel as though I go with the flow of things.
____ I can sense when I am in flow.
____ I purposely relax when working so I enter the flow experience.
____ I am aware of creative expression flowing within me.
____ I seek out quiet relaxing settings so my creativity can be maximized.
____ I seek out and enjoy relaxed, spontaneous sessions with others.
____ I quiet myself, focus myself and relax so the flow can begin.
____ When in flow I seek to continue with what I am working on until it is completed.
____ I do not begin working until I sense the flow experience.
____ I tackle projects when I sense them flowing within me.
____ As I practice living in the flow experience, I sense it operating more readily and easily within me.
____ I understand that all that lasts comes out of the flow experience.

CONCLUDING PRAYER:

"Lord, may the meditative pose become a way of life for me."

Stage One - Conception

The Holy Spirit will come upon you and the power of the most high will overshadow you; and you will conceive. (Luke 1:35, 31)

Chapter 5

Filling the First Sense of Man's Spirit by Hearing the Voice of God

Introduction

Spirit-born creativity begins and ends with the supernatural movement of God. God initiates heart faith by sending forth His Spirit to **speak** into our hearts, and God culminates His spoken word through the mighty movement of His Spirit, bringing forth supernatural fulfillment of His promises. So Spirit-born creativity both begins and ends in God, yet there are several ways in which we participate. First and foremost, we participate by becoming still and listening, (as we discussed in the last chapter). As we then hear His Word, we incubate His Word within our hearts and wait upon Him to supernaturally fulfill it.

In this chapter, we shall examine this process of releasing Spirit-born creativity, examining both God's role and man's role, so that each of us may cooperate with God in the bringing

	SENSE	HOW USED	BIBLE EXAMPLE	STAGE
1.	**Inner Ear (Jn 5:30)**	**Receives God's Rhema**	**Gen 12:1-3**	CONCEPTION
2.	Inner Eye (Rev 4:1)	Receives God's Vision	Gen 15:5,6	
3.	Inner Mind (Lk 2:19)	Ponders God's Thoughts	Rom 4:20,21	INCUBATION
4	Inner Will (Acts 19:21)	Speaks on God's Rhema	Gen 17:5	
5.	Inner Emotions (1 Kings 21:5)	Acts on God's Rhema And Vision	Gen 17:23	
	END RESULT	Death of the Vision "I" am unable to Bring it about	Gen 16:2 Gen 17:18,19	BIRTH
		Supernatural resurrection of the Vision. "In the fullness of Time GOD brings it forth."	Gen 21:1,2 Gal 4:4a	

forth of His divine purposes in our lives and in the world around us.

Abraham — An Example

Abraham is an example of one who's faith for creative feats was built upon the spoken word of God within his heart. Abraham's faith released the supernatural power of God into his personal life and has affected the world through all consecutive ages. The conception of his faith occurred when God began to speak into his heart. Record in the following space the words God spoke to Abraham. Write out Genesis 12:1-3.

You Too Can Hear God's Voice

The age in which we live is so married to rationalism and cognitive, analytical thought that it almost makes us mock when we hear of one actually claiming to be able to hear the voice of God. However, we don't mock for several reasons. First, men and women throughout the Bible heard God's voice. Second, there are some highly effective, and reputable men and women alive today who demonstrate that they hear God's voice. Finally, there is a deep hunger within us all to commune with God and hear Him speak within our hearts.

I struggled for years as a Bible-believing, born-again Christian, trying without success to hear God's voice. I prayed, fasted, studied my Bible and listened for a voice within, all to no avail. **There was no inner voice that I could hear!** Then God had me set aside a year of my life to study, read, and experiment in the area of learning to hear God's voice. During that time God taught me **four keys that opened the door to**

two-way prayer. I have discovered that not only do they work for me, but they have worked for many thousands of Christians to whom I have taught them. Actually, 99 percent of those I have taught have broken through into two-way dialogue with God, bringing tremendous intimacy to their Christian experience and transforming their very way of living. This will happen to you also as you seek God, utilizing the following four keys. They are all found in Habakkuk 2:1,2. I encourage you read it before going on.

Key #1 —God's voice in our hearts often sounds like a flow of spontaneous thoughts. Therefore, when I tune to God, I tune to spontaneity.

The Bible says that, "The Lord answered me and said..." (Hab. 2:2). Habakkuk knew the sound of God's voice. The Bible describes it as a "still small voice." I always listened for an inner **audible** voice, and surely God can and does speak that way at times. However, I have found that for most of us, most of the time, God's inner voice comes to us as **spontaneous thoughts, visions, feelings, or impressions.** For example, hasn't each of us had the experience of driving down the road and having **a thought come to us** to pray for a certain person? We generally acknowledge this as the voice of God speaking to us to pray for that individual. My question to you is, "What did God's voice sound like as you drove in your car?" Was it an inner, audible voice, or was it a spontaneous thought that lit upon your mind? Most people will say that God's voice came to them as a spontaneous thought.

So I thought to myself, "Maybe when I listen for God's voice, what I should be listening for is a flow of spontaneous thoughts. Maybe spirit level communication is received as spontaneous thoughts, impressions, feelings, and visions." Through experimentation and feedback from thousands of others, I am now convinced that this is so.

The Bible confirms this in many ways. The definition of

"paga," the Hebrew word for intercession, is "a chance encounter," or "an accidental intersecting." As God lays people on our hearts for intercession, He does it through "paga," a chance encounter thought "accidentally" intersecting our thought processes. Therefore, when I tune to God, I tune to the chance encounter thoughts, or the spontaneous thoughts. If I am poised quietly before God in prayer, I have found that the flow of spontaneous thoughts that come are quite definitely from God.

Key #2 —I must learn to still my own thoughts and emotions, so I can sense God's flow of thoughts and emotions within me.

Habakkuk said, "I will stand on my guard post and station myself on the rampart... (Hab. 2:1)." Habakkuk knew that in order to hear God's quiet, inner, spontaneous thoughts, he had to first of all go to a quiet place and quiet his own thoughts and emotions. Psalm 46:10 encourages us, "Be still, and know that I am God." There is a deep inner knowing (spontaneous flow) in our spirit that each of us can experience when we quiet our flesh and our minds.

I have found several easy ways to quiet myself so that I can more readily pick up God's spontaneous flow. Loving God through a quiet worship song is a most effective means for many. (Note II Kings 3:15.) It is as I become still (thoughts, will, and emotions) and am poised before God that the Divine flow is realized. Therefore, after I worship quietly and then become still, I open myself for that spontaneous flow. If thoughts come to me of things I have forgotten to do, I write them down and then dismiss them. If thoughts of guilt or unworthiness come to my mind, I repent thoroughly, receive the washing of the blood of the Lamb, and put on His robe of righteousness, seeing myself spotless before the presence of God.

As I fix my gaze upon Jesus (Heb. 12:2), becoming quiet in

His presence, and sharing with Him what is on my heart, I find that two-way dialogue begins to flow. Spontaneous thoughts flow from the throne of God, and I find that I am actually conversing with the King of Kings.

It is very important that one become still and properly focused if he is going to receive the pure word of God. If he is not still, he will simply be receiving his own thoughts. If he is not properly focused on Jesus, he will receive an impure flow, because the intuitive flow comes out of that upon which one has fixed his eyes. Therefore, if you have fixed your eyes upon Jesus, the intuitive flow comes from Jesus. If you have fixed your gaze upon some desire of your heart, the intuitive flow comes out of that desire of your heart. To have a pure flow, one must first of all "become still" and secondly, carefully "fix his eyes upon Jesus." Again I will say, this is quite easily accomplished by quietly worshiping the King and then receiving out of the stillness that follows.

Key #3 — As I pray, I fix the eyes of my heart upon Jesus, seeing in the spirit the dreams and visions of Almighty God.

We have already alluded to this principle in the previous paragraphs. However, we need to develop it further. Habakkuk said, "I will keep watch to see," and God said, "Record the vision (Hab. 2:1,2)." It is very interesting that Habakkuk was going to actually start looking for vision as he prayed. He was going to open the eyes of his heart and look into the spirit world to see what God wanted to show him. This is an intriguing idea.

I had never thought of opening the eyes of my heart and looking for vision. However, the more I thought of it, the more I realized that was exactly what God intended me to do. He gave me eyes in my heart. They are not to be used for lust, or visualizing failure. They are to be used to see in the spirit world the vision and movement of Almighty God.

Theologically, I believe there is an active spirit world functioning all around me. It is full of angels, demons, the Holy Spirit, the omnipresent God, and His omnipresent Son, Jesus. There is no reason for me not to see it, other than my rational culture telling me not to believe it's even there, and not instructing me on how to become open to seeing it.

The most obvious prerequisite to seeing is that we need **to look.** Daniel was seeing a vision **in his mind** and he said, "I was looking... I kept looking... I kept looking (Dan. 7:1,9,13 NASB)." Now as I pray I look for Jesus present with me, and I watch Him as He speaks to me, doing and saying the things that are on His heart. Many Christians will find that if they will only look, they will see. Jesus is Immanuel, God with us. It is as simple as that. You will see a spontaneous inner vision in a similar manner to the way you receive spontaneous inner thoughts. You can see Christ present with you in a comfortable setting, **because Christ is present with you in a comfortable setting**. Actually, you will discover that such vision comes so easily that you will have a tendency to reject it, thinking that it is just you. (Doubt is satan's most effective weapon against the Church.) However, if you will persist in recording these visions your doubt will soon be overcome by faith, as you recognize that the content of them could only be birthed in Almighty God.

God continually revealed Himself to His covenant people using dream and vision. He did so from Genesis to Revelation, saying that since the Holy Spirit was poured out in Acts 2, we should expect to receive a continuing flow of dreams and visions (Acts 2:1-4). Jesus, our Perfect Example, demonstrated this ability by living out of ongoing contact with Almighty God. He said that He did nothing on his own initiative, but only that which He **saw the Father doing, and heard the Father saying**. (Jn. 5:19,20,30) What an incredible way to live!

Is it actually possible for us to live out of the Divine initiative as Jesus did? I believe it is. A major purpose of

Jesus's death and resurrection was that the veil was torn from top to bottom, and now we all have access into the immediate presence of God and are commanded to draw near (Heb. 10:19-22). Therefore, even though what I am describing seems a bit unusual to a rational 20th century culture, it is demonstrated and described as being a **central biblical teaching and experience**. It is time to restore to the Church that which belongs to the Church.

Some, because of their intense rational nature and because of their existence in an overly rational culture, will need more assistance with and understanding of these truths before they can move into them. They will find this help in the book **Dialogue With God** by the same author.

Key #4 — Journaling, the writing out of our prayers and God's answers, provides a great new freedom in hearing God's voice.

God told Habakkuk to "record the vision and inscribe it on tablets... (Hab. 2:2)." It had never crossed my mind to write out my prayers and God's answers, as Habakkuk did. Actually, it was commanded by God. If you begin to search Scripture for this idea, you will find hundreds of chapters demonstrating it (Psalms, many of the prophets, Revelation). Why, then, hadn't I ever thought of it? Why hadn't I ever heard a sermon on it?

I decided to call the process journaling and began to experiment with it. I discovered it was a fabulous facilitator in clearly discerning God's inner, spontaneous flow, because as I journaled I was able **to write in faith for long periods of time,** simply believing it was God. I did not have to test it as I was receiving it (which jams one's receiver), because I knew that when the flow was over I could go back and test and examine it carefully **at that time**, making sure that it lined up with Scripture.

You will be amazed as you attempt journaling. Doubt may

hinder you at first, but throw it off, reminding yourself that it is a biblical concept, and that God is present speaking to His children. Don't take yourself too seriously. Play it like a game. When you take yourself too seriously, you become tense and in the way of the Holy Spirit's movement. It is when we cease **our labors** and enter His rest that God is free to flow (Heb. 4:10). Therefore, put a smile on your face, sit back comfortably, get out your pen and paper, turn your attention toward God in praise and worship, and seek His face. As you write out your question to God and become still, fixing your gaze on Jesus Who is present there with you, you will suddenly have a very good thought in response to your question. Don't doubt it, simply write it down. Later, as you go over your journaling, you will be amazed to discover that you are dialoguing with God.

Some final notes. No one should attempt this who has not read through at least the New Testament (preferably the entire Bible). In addition, one should be submitted to solid spiritual leadership. All major directional moves that come through journaling should first be submitted to those over you in the Lord before being acted upon. It is **highly recommended** that before pursuing the techniques described above, the reader more thoroughly acquaint himself with them by reading the entire book **Dialogue With God** by the same author. May the experience of Habakkuk be yours. A specialized journal is also available for Christians, providing them with many helps.

God's Voice Births God's Creativity Within Man

God's creativity begins with His voice which often comes as a thought He places within our minds. This thought frequently comes as a **spontaneous thought or idea**. Therefore, it becomes important for us to tune to spontaneity as we seek that creative flow. When a thought comes floating through our minds, it is wise to give it the time of day, because it may be worth more than we can imagine.

Testing the Inner Voice

To help insure that the flow is pure, we need to fix our eyes upon Jesus as we tune to spontaneity. The following chart will assist you in testing this flow of ideas to make sure that you are tuning into God.

Since God's voice often comes to us as an intuitive, subjective experience, it needs to be carefully tested. First, we are to examine it in light of Scripture. We need to test its origin, its content, and its fruit. The following chart will assist you in testing this flow of ideas to make sure that you are tuning into God.

Self	Satan	God
Find its origin. (Test the spirit - I Jn. 4:1.)		
Born in meditation. A progressive building of ideas.	A flashing mental thought. Was mind empty, idle? Does thought seem obstructive?	Sensed in innermost being. Then formed in thoughts. Was mind focused on Jesus?
Examine its content. (Test the words - I Jn. 4:5.)		
A consideration of things I have learned.	Negative, destructive, pushy, fearful, accusative, violates nature of God. Violates Word. Thought is afraid to be tested.	Instructive, upbuilding, comforting. Thought accepts testing.
See its fruit. (Test the fruit - Matt. 7:15,16.)		
Variable	Fear, compulsion, bondage, anxiety, . confusion	Quickens faith, powerful, brings peace, good fruit, enlightenment, knowledge.

The fruit of inner spiritual experiences should be an increase in love, reconciliation, healing, and wholeness.

All revelations calling for any kind of a major change or

decision in your life should be submitted to the body of Christ, specifically, to your spiritual overseer, for confirmation and/or adjustment. This is a safeguard God has given us. A spiritual overseer provides a protective covering for us, keeping us from being confused and/or destroyed by either self's or satan's subjective, intuitive experiences.

The Bible tells us to submit ourselves to one another (Eph. 5:21), especially to those who keep watch over our souls (Heb. 13:17). In the mouth of two or three witnesses every fact is to be confirmed. I find it best to be submitted to three individuals at all times. If there is an exceptionally major decision being made in my life, I lay what I have heard from God before them, asking them to pray and see what God would say to them. I make it a policy to wait until there is unity among the four of us before I act. This has provided an excellent protective covering in my life for over ten years.

Establishing Spiritual Coverings in Your Life

When establishing a spiritual covering in your life, realize first of all that God has already put some of them in place, for instance, your husband, your pastor, your employer. In addition to these, you may desire to establish additional covering (with the consent of those God has already placed in your life as a covering). If so, you will need to pray for God to reveal who this person should be. He should be a person who (1) knows the Bible, (2) can hear God's voice, (3) is a friend, (4) is himself submitted to others, and (5) is willing to enter into this relationship with you.

Watching Your Vision — Three Possible Focuses

When tuning to spontaneity, it is important to be aware of where you have fixed your eyes. If you are looking inward to yourself, the flow will be coming from your own heart. If you are looking at the issue, the flow will be coming from the issue.

If you are looking to Jesus, the flow will be coming from Jesus. The principle is that the intuitive flow comes from that which we fix our eyes upon. That is why it is so important to fix our eyes upon Jesus. If you have a problem to present to Him, see Him meeting the problem. Watch what He does and says, and then you will have a pure answer from the throne of grace.

Reviewing Levels of Creativity

The least creative person will be the one who has not yet discovered spontaneous flow. He is still living in the reasonings of his mind. The next highest level of creativity is in the one who has learned to live out of instinct, intuition, and spontaneity. The highest level of creativity is in the one who has learned to fix his gaze upon Jesus (Heb. 12:2) while he tunes to spontaneity. This one will exhibit the creativity of Almighty God.

Do not be satisfied to have only the creativity of man's heart. Receive the creativity of God's heart.

Being Stretched by God

God says that His ways are not our ways and His thoughts are not our thoughts. Therefore, when we come to His voice, we often discover that He would have us do things differently than we may assume would be right. He would have us give attention to things to which we thought we had already given enough attention. At times, He will call us to do things which seem bizarre. However, it is always right and best to receive His instructions and goals for our lives — for every area of our lives.

On the following journaling exercise please fill in the instructions of Jesus for each area of life you bring before Him.

Goal-setting Through Journaling

Dear Lord Jesus, what are the goals You would like me to focus on at this time?

In my family life...

In my spiritual walk...

In my work...

In caring for my health/body...

In interpersonal relationships...

In finances...

In ministry...

Intensive Journaling Worksheet

In this worksheet, you will ask God about a specific problem or goal to which He would have you give special attention during this study. After receiving His response to the first question, you will then journal through the remaining questions, which will provide you with insight into His response.

1. Lord, would You state clearly and specifically a goal You would like to achieve in me within the next six months (or an area you would like me to work on)?

2. Lord, why do You want me to achieve this goal (or focus on this area)?

3. Lord, if I succeed, what will be the result?

4. Lord, what will You consider to be a moderate success? A good success? A tremendous success? Please be specific.

5. Lord, talk to me about Your desire for my achievement of this goal.

6. Lord, how will achieving this goal contribute to the long range goals You have for my life?

7. What will it cost me to achieve this goal?

8. Lord, what will happen if I'm not successful?

9. Lord, what are the major steps involved in achieving this goal? Is there a target date for each step?

10. What obstacles stand between me and the successful completion of this project? How will they be overcome?

11. What do you want me to do today that will start me on the path to achieving this goal?

12. Lord, please give me a clear vision of this goal. (Write down the vision God gives you.)

Being Stretched by Man: the Brainstorming Process

Not only do we allow God to stretch us, but we also allow man to stretch us. In a multitude of counselors there is safety. We need both **Christ** and the **body** of Christ. Neither takes the place of the other.

You ask, "Well, why can't God just speak directly to me? Why do I need to go to imperfect human vessels?" Good questions. I believe that part of the answer is found in the fact that **often we have a very limited focus**. We look at a problem from only one angle, and we have such tunnel vision, and such a strong fixation of focus, that it is practically impossible for God to get through with any direction of His own without doing something drastic like putting us into a trance, which, scripturally, we do not see happening that often.

God, therefore, has given us each other, and probably one of the best methods for the stretching of one individual's vision and widening his perspective is the group process called brainstorming.

The Concept of Brainstorming

1. A brainstorming session is simply a creative meeting whose single purpose is to produce a list of ideas which can **later** be evaluated and processed as possible solutions to problems.
2. The greatest value of brainstorming is that it can provide more good ideas in less time than a conventional meeting.

Fundamental Rules for Brainstorming

1. Judgment and criticism are forbidden.
2. Freewheeling is welcomed.
3. Go for quantity.
4. Seek to combine and improve ideas as they are mentioned.

Additional Guidelines for Brainstorming

1. Make your problem specific, rather than general.

2. Use brainstorming only for problems that call for idea-finding, rather than judgment.
3. The ideal number of people for a brainstorming session is 12. A good length for the meeting is approximately 30 minutes.
4. Begin the brainstorming session by explaining the four basic rules given above. Put them on a chalkboard or a placard.
5. Avoid an atmosphere of perfectionism. Keep it fun.
6. Encourage ideas that are sparked by previous ideas. Encourage a chain reaction, where individuals feed creatively off the ideas of others.
7. Have a non-participant present to record every idea that is mentioned.

Why Brainstorming Works

1. Through chain reaction, you spark each others' creativity.
2. People tend to think up more ideas in a group than alone.
3. When competing to think up ideas, output can be increased by 50%.
4. Accepting all ideas rewards individuals for their behavior.

Personal Application for Classtime

Post the rules for brainstorming. Review and discuss the entire process. Then give it a try. Pick a subject that is of interest to all, not a judgment kind of issue, and not too difficult for your first try. One possibility would be "Listing as many ways as possible for improving communication within the home." One group with which I worked came up with over 100 ideas within 30 minutes. The following week, we gave each class member a copy of these ideas.

You will enjoy the relaxed, fun atmosphere of brainstorming. Use the grade sheet provided at the end of this chapter and grade yourselves when you are done.

Personal Application for Homework

If you did not complete the goal-setting through journaling that was assigned earlier, go back and finish it as part of this week's homework. You may want to take one of the goals that you journaled about, sit down, and brainstorm with several others during the week, just to become more accustomed to the brainstorming process to see where it may lead you as you work through a particular goal. Record below any insights, observations and questions from this chapter. Also, read Genesis 12:1 through 22:19. Briefly acquaint yourself with the entire story of the development of Abraham's faith. You may wish to jot down the flow of major events.

Returning to Journaling After Brainstorming

Brainstorming will give you many ideas which will have to be weeded out. One excellent place to weed these out is in your journal. You can take them and present them before the Lord and see what He has to say about them. He will tell you which ones to drop and which ones to work with. **Caution:** Make sure that you do not focus exclusively on the item you are bringing to the Lord. Set the item down before the Lord, and **focus your attention on the Lord**. Then you will receive a pure answer concerning the item.

Also, if you have brainstormed in class on improving communication in the home, you may want to journal and work with one or several of the ideas that were presented in the classroom.

Two Variations of the Brainstorming Process

There are several variations of the Brainstorming process which we could examine. However, we will share only two at this time. The first we shall call "branching out" and the second is called "storyboarding."

1. Branching Out

In this variation of the brainstorming process, rather than simply listing your ideas with your topic on the top of the page, you begin by placing it in the middle of the page (or blackboard) in a small circle. When you think of a related idea you draw a spoke-like line out from the center, and write the idea and circle it. The second idea may spark two or three related thoughts; if so, you draw more spokes out from the second circle and include the newest thoughts. Then you go back to the main idea and brainstorm again from there. By the time you are done your paper may look like this:

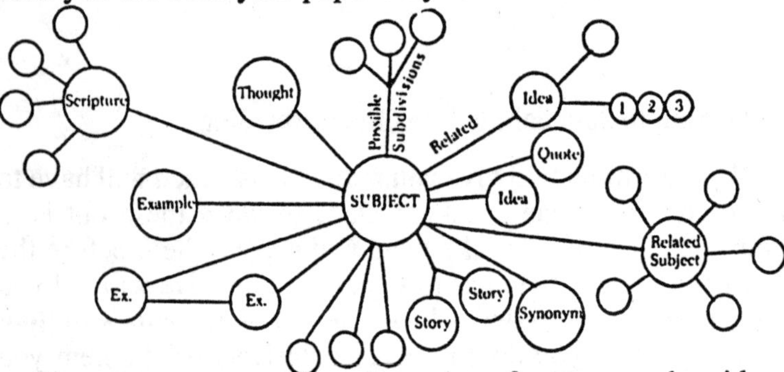

You may even want to center some of your secondary ideas on separate sheets and brainstorm from them.

As with the brainstorm lists, you want to jot down everything that comes to mind. But there are at least two advantages to this newer technique. First, the visual layout helps your thinking to go in a variety of directions; and second, related ideas can be easily grouped together as you go, no matter what order you think of them. Organization into a more linear outline can easily be done later.

Once the brainstorming process is completed, you will want to prayerfully select the ideas, scriptures, stories, examples, etc., that you sense are bearing witness within your heart, and begin working with these.

2. Storyboarding

Storyboarding is another variation of the brainstorming process. The storyboard is an excellent planning tool because it helps visualize the parts of the plan as they are being formulated. It was first used in the movie industry to help lay out the sequence of scenes for a film. The storyboard is now used by hotel and restaurant chains, various corporations, educational institutions, and international Christian organizations. The storyboard serves the planning process in the following ways:

— It aids the brainstorming process.
— It helps keep attention on the topic under discussion.
— It helps organize functions and activities in proper sequence.
— It stimulates innovation and creativity.

The storyboard resembles a bulletin board. It can be constructed out of cork or any material that allows pins to be stuck in it easily. The storyboard can be any size, the larger the better. Many organizations cover an entire wall with cork.

Three basic card sizes are needed when using a storyboard. The largest card (an 8 ½ x 11 sheet of typing paper) is used for the topic card. The next largest card (approximately 5 x 7) is used for the major heading being discussed or planned. The smaller card (3 x 5) is used to record subpoint activities for each of the headings (see diagram).

Using the basic rules described previously for brainstorming,

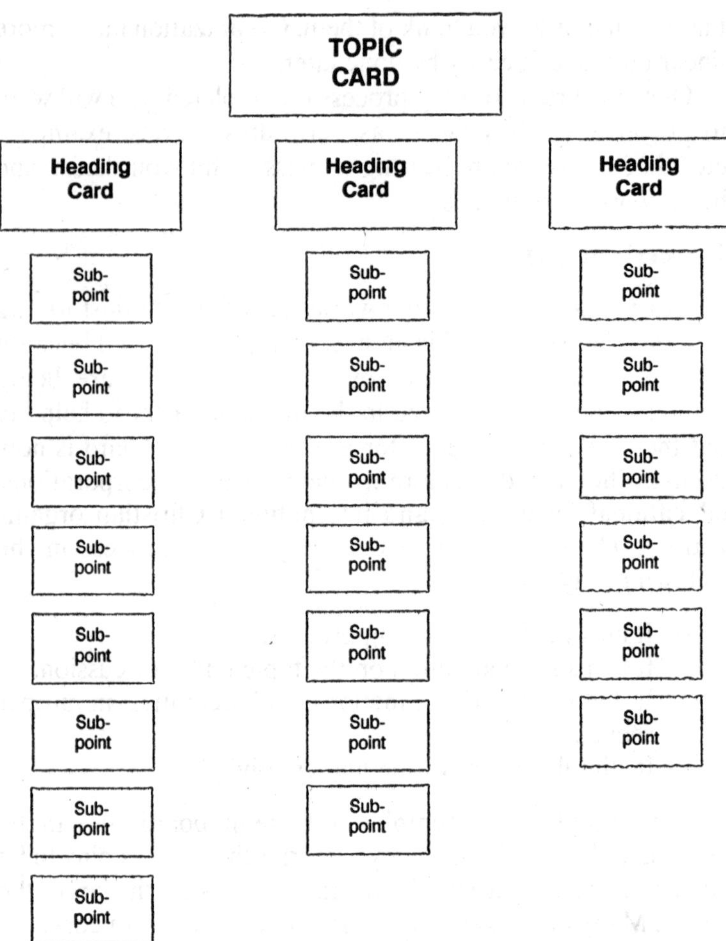

The storyboard resembles a bulletin board in design. Cards are pinned on the board showing the topic being discussed or planned. Heading cards show the major being discussed and sub-point cards show the various activities under each function.

individuals or small groups of individuals begin bringing up cards and posting them in their appropriate place on the board. Remember you are going for quantity. Quality will be examined later. During the brainstorming session, the ideas are written on the appropriate card (topic, heading, or subpoint) and placed on the storyboard as shown in the accompanying diagram.

Once the brainstorming session is over, each idea on the storyboard is evaluated in terms of its validity, order of sequence, and location in the plan. Those ideas determined invalid are removed from the storyboard. The location of others may need to be changed, depending on where they fit in the overall plan.

Idea for Classroom Activity During the Next Few Weeks

As a class experiment you may want to use these processes by picking a topic for brainstorming and developing the ideas on the blackboard or storyboard. Remember it is best to pick a topic which is of interest to all concerned. Suggestions include, "How to handle rebellious children," or "How to increase your child's commitment to the Lord," or for all spouses, "How to make love last forever." Please feel free to add other topics of general interest to this list for use during classtime in the weeks to come.

A Personal Experience

Since this chapter is on filling the first sense of one's spirit by hearing the voice of God, let me share a personal example of how God's spoken word has granted me heart faith during a difficult period of transition.

A group of men from the church I was pastoring approached me with a written request, asking me to step down as pastor for a six-week period while the church sought to resolve some difficulties among us. As I sought the Lord concerning this, He spoke to me that He would not release me from the position of responsibility over the church, and that I was not to step down. Upon receiving confirmation from my spiritual overseers, I walked in that Rhema.

As storms brewed around me I found the next six weeks to be the greatest six week period of insight into the Word that I have ever had in my life. God opened the Scripture in unbelievable ways before me, laying a foundation of truth which I shall use the rest of my life. These truths are also greatly affecting those with whom I share them. Some of these truths are being shared in this manual.

After the six weeks were over, God continued to speak to me to continue as pastor, even though in the flesh I would have preferred to resign. However, about two months later, as healing and restoration were taking place, God told me to resign. Upon receiving confirmation from my spiritual overseers, I did. With no other work before me, I found myself in the hands of God. God spoke that He would open up a teaching ministry before me. Over the successive months I watched in amazement as God performed what no human could have performed. He offered me my heart's desire in the teaching ministry. God's Rhema truly granted the wisdom and grace to lead me prosperously through a difficult transition time in my life.

Personal Application Checklist When Brainstorming

Rules for teaming up: (Answer yes or no.)

____ 1. There's an incentive for all involved.
____ 2. We set aside a time and place to think.
____ 3. The meeting and thinking time was fun and informal.
____ 4. After thinking together we went back and thought alone.
____ 5. We met again and chose a satisfactory solution.
____ 6. We did not argue.

____ 7. We began the brainstorming session by explaining the following four basic rules. We put them on a chalk board or a placard.

(Judgment and criticism are forbidden. Freewheeling is welcomed. Go for quantity. Seek to combine and improve ideas as they are mentioned.)

____ 8. We made the problem specific, rather than general.

____ 9. The problems we selected for brainstorming called for idea-finding, rather than judgment.

____ 10. We kept the group to about 12, and the time to about 30 minutes.

____ 11. We avoided an atmosphere of perfectionism. We kept it fun.

____ 12. We encouraged ideas that were sparked by previous ideas.

____ 13. We had a non-participant present to record every idea that was mentioned.

FUNDAMENTAL RULES FOR BRAINSTORMING:

1. **JUDGMENT AND CRITICISM ARE FORBIDDEN.**
2. **FREEWHEELING IS WELCOMED.**
3. **GO FOR QUANTITY.**
4. **SEEK TO COMBINE AND IMPROVE IDEAS.**

Chapter 6

Filling the Second Sense of Man's Spirit by Seeing the Vision of God

Crystallizing the Voice of God with a Vision from God

The **second** faculty of our hearts which serves as a primary channel for receiving the revelation of God is the "eyes of our heart (Eph. 1:18)." Even as our physical eyes are a primary sense in receiving information from the physical world, so our spiritual eyes are a primary sense used by God to give us revelation from the spiritual world. From Genesis to Revelation, God gave dreams and visions to those who sought Him. These dreams and visions constitute a vital ingredient in the forming of heart faith.

In the development of faith within Abraham's life, God added to the spoken word He had given him; He gave him a vision of the promise fulfilled. Write out Gen. 15:1,5,6.

	SENSE	HOW USED	BIBLE EXAMPLE	STAGE
1.	Inner Ear (Jn 5:30)	Receives God's Rhema	Gen 12:1-3	CONCEPTION
2.	**Inner Eye (Rev 4:1)**	**Receives God's Vision**	**Gen 15:5,6**	
3.	Inner Mind (Lk 2:19)	Ponders God's Thoughts	Rom 4:20,21	INCUBATION
4	Inner Will (Acts 19:21)	Speaks on God's Rhema	Gen 17:5	
5.	Inner Emotions (1 Kings 21:5)	Acts on God's Rhema And Vision	Gen 17:23	
	END RESULT	Death of the Vision "I" am unable to Bring it about	Gen 16:2 Gen 17:18,19	BIRTH
		Supernatural resurrection of the Vision. "In the fullness of Time GOD brings it forth."	Gen 21:1,2 Gal 4:4a	

God knew that a picture or vision would deepen and solidify the previously spoken rhema word [1], and so He added to the spoken word a vision of the promise fulfilled. God gave Abraham an external vision: the stars of the sky and the sands of the sea. As the Apostle John wrote Revelation, God gave him inner visions. These two examples illustrate that God can give either internal or external visions.

In either case, I believe that the receiving of vision is a necessary ingredient for developing heart faith. I believe that along with rhema, God wants to give dreams and visions which will deepen and solidify the rhema word.

When an architect is going to design a new building, he first begins with an idea — rhema, if you will. Next, he pictures the building in his mind. **Then** he is ready to begin creating.

Nothing exists which has not first been seen in someone's mind. Seeing is a prerequisite to creating. Scientists have discovered that two groups of people use imagery a great deal: geniuses and children, both of whom are very creative. Albert Einstein stated, "Imagination is more important than knowledge." Shakespeare said, "Imagination makes man the paragon of animals." Disraeli declared, "Imagination governs the world." Aristotle, the founder of formal logic, showed the centrality of thinking with the use of images when he wrote, "It is impossible even to think without a mental picture."

The Fourth Dimension Created the Third Dimension.

"By faith we understand that the worlds were prepared by the rhema (Greek) of God, so that what is seen, is not made out of things which are visible (Heb. 11:3)."

I believe that God saw the visible world within His Spirit and then created the three-dimensional world out of the vision

---

1 For a brief study on rhema as the "spoken word of God," see Appendix A.

incubated within His heart. Whatever is incubated in the fourth dimension, which is the spirit world, is produced in the third dimension.

Jesus, Our Pattern, Lived Constantly Tuned to Vision.

Jesus, lived His earthly life out of rhema and vision. "The things which I **heard** from Him, these things I speak... (Jn. 8:26)."

"I speak the things which I have **seen** in the presence of my father... (Jn. 8:38)."

"I do **nothing on my own initiative**, but I speak these things as the Father taught me (John 8:28)."

We too must come to living moment by moment out of the rhema and vision of God. In this manner, we will flow with the Father's initiative and walk as Christ walked.

Creative Change Occurs by Seeing the Unseen.

The Bible tells us how we can bring **creative changes** into our lives and the world around us. Write out II Corinthians 3:18 and 4:17,18.

One is **transformed** by **looking persistently** at the invisible spiritual realm. If we look persistently at the things that are seen, we will not be creative. If we look with our inner eye at the invisible, spiritual realm and incubate the spiritual vision that God gives within our hearts, God will deliver it forth in the fullness of His time into the third dimensional world.

Consider the miracle of Peter walking on the water as an example. The story is found in Matthew 14:28-32. Jesus spoke rhema by telling Peter to come to Him on the water. Peter acted in faith, stepping over the edge of the boat. Peter "saw vision" by fixing his eyes upon the supernatural provision of God being displayed in Jesus. A miracle occurred. Creative power was released into Peter's life; he walked on water. However, the miracle was aborted, because instead of continuing to look at Jesus and the supernatural provision of God, Peter **looked at the visible realm**. Immediately the supernatural flow ceased and Peter began to sink. Thus, creative supernatural energies are released **while we look** not at the things seen, but at the things **not** seen.

God gives us supernatural vision so that as we gaze upon it, His supernatural energy may flow into our lives. "We walk by faith, not by appearance (II Cor. 5:7)."

> **The place you fix your eyes and the place you tune your ears will determine whether or not you have heart faith.**

"Fixing our eyes on Jesus, the author and perfecter of faith... (Heb. 12:2)"

Learning to Present the Eyes of Our Heart to God

The Hebrew word for prophet means "seer." A prophet is a "seer," one who sees the visions and purposes of God.

In II Kings 6:8-23, we read the story of Elisha and his stand against the Armenians. As they encircled Elisha's dwelling, his servant feared, looking only at the visible situation. However, Elisha saw with spiritual eyes into the spiritual realm. When he prayed for the Lord to open his servant's eyes, the servant also saw that the mountain all around Elisha was full of horses and chariots of fire.

We need to learn to see the invisible realm, rather than simply the visible realm. We need to be trained up in the "school of the prophets" so we, too, become seers. To start with, we must learn to still ourselves and focus on God. Instead of believing that our inner eye is only good for vain imaginations and daydreams, we must see that we can present it moment by moment to God and, by doing so, have it filled with supernatural dream and vision.

Habakkuk went to his place of prayer to **keep watch to see** what God would speak to him, and God gave him a **vision** to write down and refer to (Hab. 2:1,2). Habakkuk, "a seer," had learned to present his inner eyes to God as he prayed, so that he could receive God's dream and vision.

The Apostle John also presented his inner eyes to God as he waited to receive God's voice and vision. Write out Revelation 4:1,2 from the NASB or the Amplified.

May I suggest that in verse one of Revelation 4, John is "priming the pump." He is presenting his inner eye to the spiritual realm, "looking" to see if God wants to give him a vision. And sure enough, God does. In verse two, he is taken "in the spirit" to see a vision of the throne room. It is interesting to note that he is not caught up in the Spirit **until verse two**, which makes one wonder where John is in verse 1, if he is not yet caught up in the spirit, and what John is doing.

Now what is significant, I believe, is that we can **"prime the pump"** by **looking**. For years I totally disregarded the inner eye, believing it consisted of simple imaginations, which were worthless. I never received visions from God. Now, as I present my inner eye to God to be filled by Him, I find constant spiritual vision flowing within me. This can happen to each of us, and as it does, we will begin to be trained up in the school of the prophets.

The following suggestions provide opportunities for you to begin being open to God, allowing Him to fill the eyes of your heart with His dream and vision.

1. You need to "be still" outwardly and inwardly so the Holy Spirit can issue forth with a flow of living images.
2. Enter a Bible story, using vision. This is probably the most common way of all. Simply allow yourself to see what you are reading. And you can do more than just see the scenes. As you are seeing them, ask God to show you what He wants to show you, and a flow of inner images directed by God can take over.
3. Open the eyes of your heart during your quiet times, allowing God to show you things. I have found that focusing intently upon Jesus until He begins moving or speaking prompts the flow of the Holy Spirit's images (Heb. 12:2).
4. In intercession for others, see the person you are praying for, and then see Christ meeting that person. Watch what He does, then pray that into existence.
5. Listen to your dreams, which are a natural expression of the inner world. Ask God to speak to you during the night (Ps. 127:2). When you awaken, **immediately** record your dreams, and then ask God for an interpretation. He will give it.
6. Praying in the spirit opens up communication with the Holy Spirit and allows images to arise, especially if you are presenting the eyes of your heart to God.
7. Quiet prayer, simply affirming your love for Jesus and His love toward you, opens you to reflections and insights which are a form of imagination in action.
8. During praise and worship, see what you are singing and allow the Holy Spirit to carry the vision where He wants.

Seeing Vision — Personal Application

Please answer the following questions briefly. (If your visionary capacity appears blocked for some reason, please turn to Appendix B, "Allowing God to Restore Your Visionary Capacity.")

1. Do you generally ask God for a vision of the goals He has placed in your heart?

2. Are you generally aware of the pictures that are flowing within your mind?

3. Do you generally take steps to guide or control the pictures that flow within your mind?

4. Have you grown accustomed to the flow of divine visions within your heart and mind?

5. How powerful do you feel the pictures are in your mind?

Suggested Books on Using our Visionary Capacity in Encountering God

1. For a description of the practical ways Dr. Paul Yonggi Cho lives, pregnant with the dream and vision, read his book, **The Fourth Dimension.**
2. For a good book describing the use of imagery in the ministry of inner healing read **Healing Life's Hurts,** by Fathers Dennis and Matt Linn.

Testing Dream and Vision

Since dreams and visions may flow from your spirit, the Holy Spirit or satan, they need to be carefully tested against the Word. Major ones should be submitted to your spiritual counselor. The following diagram, although practically identical to the one in the previous chapter, is presented for your review, and as a guide to help you test your dreams and visions.

ONE INNER SCREEN — THREE PROJECTORS

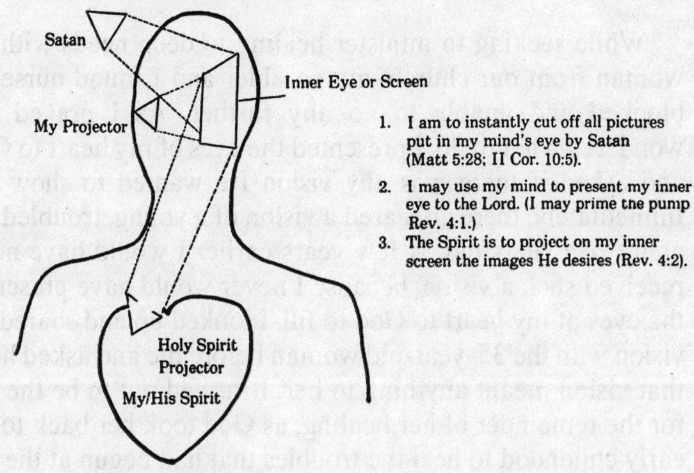

TESTING WHETHER AN IMAGE IS FROM SELF, SATAN OR GOD

SELF	SATAN	GOD
	Find Its Origin (Test the Spirit — I Jn. 4:1)	
Born in mind. A painting of a picture.	A flashing image. Was mind empty, idle? Does image seem obstructive?	A living flow of pictures coming from the innermost being. Was your inner being quietly focused on Jesus?
	Examining Its Content (Test the Ideas — I Jn. 4:5)	
A painting of things I have learned.	Negative, destructive, pushy, fearful, accusative, violates nature of God. Violates Word of God. Image is afraid to be tested. Ego appeal.	Instructive, upbuilding, comforting. Image accepts testing.
	Seeing Its Fruit (Test the Fruit — Matt. 7:15)	
Variable	Fear, compulsion, bondage, anxiety, confusion. Inflated ego.	Quickens faith, powerful, peace, good fruit, enlightenment, knowledge. Produces humility.

A Personal Illustration of God's Vision Filling the Eyes of the Heart

While seeking to minister healing to deep needs within a woman from our church, my co-elder and I found ourselves blocked and unable to go any further. As I prayed and wondered what to do, I presented the eyes of my heart to God, and asked if there was any vision He wanted to show me. Immediately, there appeared a vision of a young, troubled girl about five years old. A few years earlier I would have never received such a vision, because I never would have presented the eyes of my heart to God to fill. I looked up and shared the vision with the 35-year-old woman before me and asked her if that vision meant anything to her. It turned out to be the key for the remainder of her healing, as God took her back to her early childhood to heal the troubles that had begun at the age of five years.

The vision of God can give the heart wisdom and strength to act in faith and see supernatural results.

My wife and I have had numerous visions which we have incubated for months and even years. Some have been beautifully fulfilled and some are still being incubated. One of my wife's visions has been to live in a beautiful large old house. I knew that as a pastor of a small rural congregation that was impossible in the natural. Finances would just not allow such a thing. However, when our church purchased property on which to build, the property had a beautiful, large, old house, which in earlier days had been the social center of our town. It was a fulfillment even beyond her dreams as we moved into it. God's vision, incubated over the years, had brought a miracle into our lives, granting even the desires of my wife's heart.

Personal Application — Goal-setting Through Recording God's Visions

In the last chapter, you went through the following

questions, asking God to speak to you concerning each of them. Now go back through them, this time asking God to couple a clear vision with each of His goals for your life. As you ask for vision, **look for vision**. You will find it appearing. Write a brief description of each vision as you see it. Look for a vision for each of the following questions. You may want to review the answer to each question that God gave you in the last chapter just before asking for an accompanying vision. Then, with your heart primed with God's rhema word to you, **look to see**.

Dear Lord Jesus, please show me a vision of the goals You would like me to focus on at this time. Pause to look for a picture in your mind (Daniel 7) and then record a summary of it, or describe it.

In my family life...

In my spiritual walk...

In my work...

In caring for my health/body...

In interpersonal relationships...

In finances...

In ministry...

Intensive Journaling Worksheet for Recording Vision

In this worksheet, you will ask God about a specific problem or goal to which He would have you give special attention during this semester. After receiving His response to the first question, you will then journal through the remaining questions, which will provide you with insight into His response. Again, **look for vision to accompany the rhema from the last chapter**. Begin by reviewing the rhema word from the last chapter.

1. Lord, would You show clearly and specifically a goal You would like to achieve in me within the next six months?

2. Lord, let me see why you want me to achieve this goal.

3. Lord, if I succeed, please show me what the result will be.

4. Lord, what will You consider to be a moderate success? A good success? A tremendous success? Please show me specifically.

5. Lord, show me about Your desire for my achievement of this goal.

6. Lord, show me how achieving this goal will contribute to the long range goals You have for my life.

7. Show me what it will cost me to achieve this goal.

8. Lord, show me what will happen if I'm not successful.

9. Lord, show me the major steps involved in achieving this goal. Is there a target date for each step?

10. Show me what obstacles stand between me and the successful completion of this project. Show me how they will be overcome.

11. Show me what You want me to do today that will start me on the path to achieving this goal.

Personal Application — Ask Questions to Spark Your Imagination

Sometimes we seem to get stuck. There seems to be no fresh flow of ideas or vision at all. At times like this you can apply the following questions to the problem or goal on which you are working. Record your reflections in the spaces provided. The following list of questions is designed to help you work through a goal or problem that is *not market-oriented. A second list* of questions is provided which is specifically designed for marketing ideas, things and projects. Select the appropriate list.

All these questions are brainstorm-oriented. They are for generating a great list of ideas and for stretching your thinking and perspectives. They will assist in releasing a fullness of your creativity and the creativity of the group. **However, this is not necessarily God's creativity.** You will need to take this list and present it before God in prayer, and while gazing at God, not the list, ask what He wants to speak into your life concerning these issues. A place for you to do this is provided at the end of the chapter.

A. Questions to Use When Dealing with Issues, Rather than Projects

(e.g., ways of healing a broken relationship, ideas for strengthening a family bond, ideas for reconciling a theological disagreement, ideas for building creative sermons)

1. State succinctly the precise subject or problem you want to think about.

2. What are the conventional ways people have handled this kind of situation?

3. What are the most unconventional approaches which you have heard of or can think of for handling this problem?

4. Picture Jesus in this situation. How would He handle it?

5. List as many biblical principles or stories or illustrations as possible which might apply to this situation.

6. What biblical principles would appear to be in tension with those which you have already listed?

7. From what totally different perspectives could you view this problem, or issue? What new ideas come from viewing the situation from this perspective?

B. Questions Specifically Designed for Marketing Business Ideas

When you are seeking creative ideas for developing and marketing a product, the following questions can spark your imagination.

1. **How can I put this to other uses?** New ways to use as is? Other uses if modified?

2. **Adapt?** What else is like this? What other ideas does this suggest? Does the past offer a parallel? What could I copy? Whom could I emulate?

3. **How could it be modified?** New twist? Change meaning, color, motion, sound, odor, form, shape? Other changes?

4. **How could this be magnified?** What to add? More time? Greater frequency? Stronger? Higher? Longer? Thicker? Extra value? Plus ingredient? Duplicate? Multiply? Exaggerate?

5. **Minimize?** What to subtract or omit? Smaller? Condensed? Miniature? Lower? Shorter? Lighter? Streamline? Split up? Understate?

6. **Substitute?** Who else instead? What else instead? Other ingredient? Other material? Other process? Other power? Other place? Other approach? Other tone of voice?

7. **Rearrange?** Interchange components? Other pattern? Other layout? Other sequence? Transpose cause and effect? Change pace? Change schedule?

8. **Reverse?** Transpose positive and negative? How about opposites? Turn it backward? Turn it upside down? Reverse roles? Change shoes? Turn tables? Turn other cheek?

9. **Combine?** How about a blend, an alloy, an assortment, an ensemble? Combine units? Combine purposes? Combine appeals? Combine ideas?

Adding Divine Clarity through Personal Journaling

Lord, speak to me concerning all these ideas and perspectives. Which ones, if any, do You want me to latch onto and work with? Which ones am I not to give attention to at this time? How do You want me to proceed? (Record what you sense the Lord speaking to you.)

Preparation for Classroom Discussion

1. Be prepared to discuss together any questions or thoughts which you have on the principles of vision. Jot them down.

2. Be prepared to discuss together any visions which God is placing within your heart. Often this kind of sharing sparks faith in the hearts of those who hear, and it brings glory to God.

3. There will be an open discussion on overcoming blocks and hindrances to receiving vision. If you are struggling in receiving vision, come prepared to discuss your struggle so some solutions can be offered. Jot down any struggles which you would like to have the class discuss.

4. Be prepared for a possible brainstorming or story-boarding session, if time permits.

Stage Two - Incubation

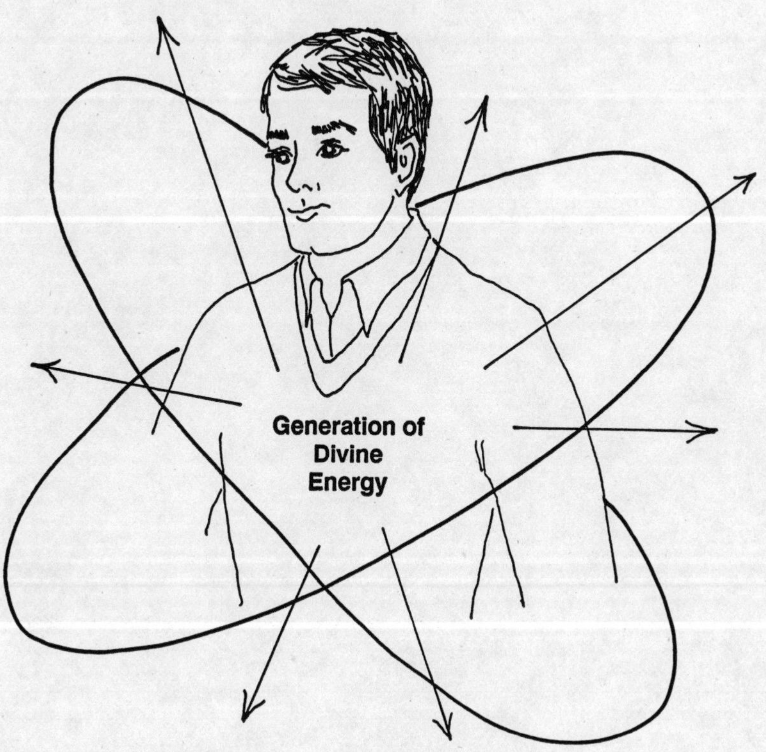

Abraham grew strong in faith
(Rom. 4:20)

Chapter 7

Filling the Third Sense of Man's Spirit by Pondering God's Voice and Vision

Introduction — The Incubation Process

Once one has received the purposes of God within his heart through the primary channels of rhema and vision, then one must begin incubating what he has seen and heard, allowing it to go around and around, filling every part of his heart. Our hearts have a mind, will and emotions which must all be saturated with the dream and vision of God. God has created us so that both our spirits (hearts) and our souls, have mind, will and emotions. Mind, will and emotions of the spirit are deeper, and have more substance than the mind, will and emotions of the soul.

For example, the heart ponders, the soul thinks. To "ponder" has a deeper connotation than to "think."

In the next three chapters we will examine these three

	SENSE	HOW USED	BIBLE EXAMPLE	STAGE
1.	Inner Ear (Jn 5:30)	Receives God's Rhema	Gen 12:1-3	CONCEPTION
2.	Inner Eye (Rev 4:1)	Receives God's Vision	Gen 15:5,6	
3.	**Inner Mind (Lk 2:19)**	**Ponders God's Thoughts**	**Rom 4:20,21**	INCUBATION
4	Inner Will (Acts 19:21)	Speaks on God's Rhema	Gen 17:5	
5.	Inner Emotions (1 Kings 21:5)	Acts on God's Rhema And Vision	Gen 17:23	
	END RESULT	Death of the Vision "I" am unable to Bring it about	Gen 16:2 Gen 17:18,19	BIRTH
		Supernatural resurrection of the Vision. "In the fullness of Time GOD brings it forth."	Gen 21:1,2 Gal 4:4a	

faculties, showing that they are faculties of the spirit, distinguishing them from their counterparts in the realm of the soul and showing how to use each one in the incubation of dream and rhema. Also, we will see that Abraham, as the "Father of Faith," allowed the dream and rhema of God to fill each of these capacities as he GREW STRONG IN FAITH (Rom. 4:20).

Discerning the Mind of the Spirit

It came as a shock to me to realize that my heart/spirit had a mind. I had known that my soul had a mind but I had never realized that my spirit also had the capacity to think deep thoughts. Let's look at a few Bible passages that tell us this.

"Mary **pondered** these things in her heart (Lk. 2:19)."

The scribes were "**reasoning** in their **hearts** (Mk. 2:6)."

These verses definitely indicate that we have the ability to ponder and reason in our hearts as well as in our souls. The guiding rule for distinguishing man's spirit from his soul is this: that which comes from the soul is external, changeable, and reactionary; that which comes from the spirit has substance, is deep and underlying (i.e., "to think" vs. "to ponder").

Filling the Mind of the Spirit

God wants us to incubate His dreams, visions, and rhemas within our hearts. He wants our inner minds to be filled with nothing but His revelation to us. If we abide in Him, and His rhema (Greek for "word") abides in us, we can ask whatever we wish (John 15:7).

God wants us to constantly live in Him, and His spoken words to live in us, so that our hearts' desires can be fully met.

Abraham **grew strong** in faith by causing his inner mind to meditate only upon God and His promises to him. Write out slowly, thoughtfully, and prayerfully, Romans 4:17-24.

Now prayerfully review what you have written and record the insights God is giving to you.

Abraham contemplated the situation (vs. 19). He was fully aware of the physical reality that was counter to the promises of God. However, he would not confess that physical reality, nor would he allow it to weaken his faith. Instead he **looked steadily at God's ability** and at God's promise, and with his thoughts would only incubate positive faith, never negative doubt. He was fully assured that what God had promised He was able also to perform. This is not written just for his sake, but that we may do the same thing.

Let's look at another biblical example, Mary, in Luke 2:8-20. Please read it now.

In verses 10-14, the angels are declaring freshly spoken rhema to the shepherds. In verse 17, the shepherds told Mary and Joseph "the **statement** (Greek word is rhema) which had been told them about the child." In verse 19, "Mary treasured all these **things** (Greek word is rhema) PONDERING them in her heart." Thus, we see Mary incubating the rhema of God in her heart, treasuring it and pondering it over and over. This is a perfect example of what we are to do in the incubation of heart faith.

One final biblical example shows the incubation process working in reverse. Take time to read the example of Elijah in I Kings 18 through 19.

After Elijah had defeated the four hundred and fifty prophets of Baal in a spectacular display of miraculous power, he was reduced to fear and retreat by a simple word of evil from Queen Jezebel. She threatened to destroy his life (19:1-3). Instead of centering down and finding the mind of the Lord, he allowed the word of destruction to enter his heart and take root, and he ran in fear, rather than standing strong in the supernatural provision of God. In so doing, he incubated evil rather than righteousness, fear rather than faith. It took God many days to restore his heart to a position where it was strong again, renewed by the freshly spoken rhema of God. God ministered to him through angels. Elijah spent forty days fasting at the mountain of the Lord (19:8) before the freshly spoken rhema of God had fully renewed his heart. As he entered into communion with God, God spoke rhema into his heart, restoring his spirit and re-commissioning him into the Lord's work (I Kings 19:13-18).

What an example this is for our lives! I know how many times it has happened to me. I have incubated evil rather than good, and destroyed my heart rather than built it up. Then I had to begin the long journey back to faith and a purified heart, renewed by the rhema of Christ.

Understanding these simple dynamics helps me stay in the love of Christ and return there more quickly when I have fallen away. I pray the same will be true in your life.

To come to heart faith we must be transformed out of the kingdom of darkness and into the kingdom of light. We must be able to recognize and destroy the working of satan while recognizing and cultivating the working of the Holy Spirit.

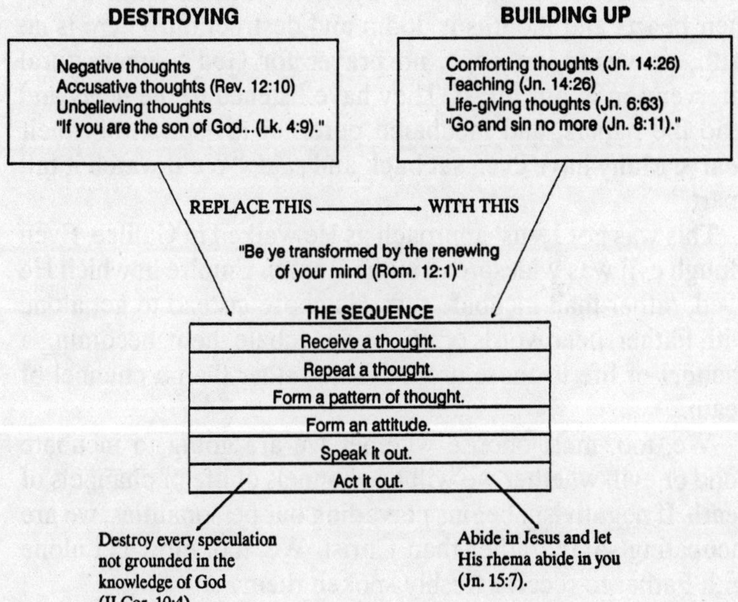

ABRAHAM - THE FATHER OF FAITH

1. HEARD THE VOICE OF THE LORD (Gen. 12:1-3)
2. SAW WITH EYES OF FAITH (Gen. 15:5,6)
3. THOUGHT WITH A HEART OF FAITH (Rom. 4:20,21)
4. SPOKE THE WORD OF FAITH (Gen. 17:5)
5. ACTED IN FAITH (Gen. 17:23)
6. RECEIVED THE PROMISE OF FAITH (Gen. 21:5)

A Personal Example

Many Christians today have a doomsday attitude toward the decline and fall of America. They have nothing good to say or believe about this great country of ours. All that comes from their hearts and mouths is doom and destruction. There is no faith, no vision, no hope, no prayer for God's supernatural intervention in our midst. They have listened to the news and read the papers, and incubated pure negativism within their hearts. Many have even sat back and said, "We'll watch it fall apart."

This was not Jesus' approach as He walked in Galilee. Even though evil was widespread in the Roman Empire in which He lived, rather than incubate that, He chose instead to get alone with Father, hear words of life, and incubate them, becoming a channel of life to those around him, rather than a channel of death.

We, too, must choose whether we are going to incubate good or evil, whether we will be channels of life or channels of death. If negativism begins pervading our personalities, we are incubating satan, rather than Christ. We, too, must get alone with Father to receive freshly spoken rhema.

For the last three years, I have prayed and fasted one day a month, for our nation. I have joined in doing this with thousands of other Christians under the leadership of "Intercessors for America." You can get their monthly newsletter from Intercessors for America, Box 1289, Elyria, Ohio 44036.

We have jointly asked forgiveness for our nations's sins, asked God to restore godly leadership, to remove abortion from the land, and to move across the land with a powerful move of His Holy Spirit. God has given me rhema and vision concerning these things as I have prayed and fasted. I have incubated those things, and I find God answering our prayers and making me a channel of life to those around me, rather than a channel of death. So may we all be in all areas of our lives. May we spend enough time each day with the Life-giver, and incubate His words of life so that we constantly speak words of life, not words of death.

May everything that is negative, accusative, and unbelieving be replaced with those things that are comforting, instructional, and life-giving. May we not incubate satan, but only the Holy Spirit in our lives.

Journaling Application

"Lord, is there any area of my life in which I am incubating negatives, rather than the word which You would like to speak to me? If so please reveal it to me and show me how you want to heal it." Record your journaled response below.

Prayer — God, may you purify our hearts with your dreams and visions.

Chapter 8

Filling the Fourth Sense of Man's Spirit by Confessing God's Rhema and Vision

Speaking from the Heart

"The mouth speaks out of that which fills the heart," said Jesus. "The good man out of his good treasure brings forth what is good; and the evil man out of his evil treasure brings forth what is evil (Matt. 12:34,35)."

We speak out of that which is in our hearts. If we have been incubating evil, we speak evil. If we have been incubating negatives, we speak negatives. If we have been incubating the voice and vision of Almighty God, we begin to speak the voice and vision of God.

Therefore, speaking becomes an important aspect of spirit-born creativity. In creating the universe, God "called into being that which does not exist (Rom. 4:17)." We must be willing to speak it forth when God instructs us to and in the

	SENSE	HOW USED	BIBLE EXAMPLE	STAGE
1.	Inner Ear (Jn 5:30)	Receives God's Rhema	Gen 12:1-3	CONCEPTION
2.	Inner Eye (Rev 4:1)	Receives God's Vision	Gen 15:5,6	
3.	Inner Mind (Lk 2:19)	Ponders God's Thoughts	Rom 4:20,21	INCUBATION
4	**Inner Will (Acts 19:21)**	**Speaks on God's Rhema**	**Gen 17:5**	
5.	Inner Emotions (1 Kings 21:5)	Acts on God's Rhema And Vision	Gen 17:23	
	END RESULT	Death of the Vision "I" am unable to Bring it about	Gen 16:2 Gen 17:18,19	BIRTH
		Supernatural resurrection of the Vision. "In the fullness of Time GOD brings it forth."	Gen 21:1,2 Gal 4:4a	

way He instructs us to. If we don't, we can prevent the creative process from being completed. The energy which has been growing within our spirits needs a channel to guide its release. Our spoken words provide that channel or form. As the creative energy from our spirits is released, it fills the form made for it by the words of our mouth. For example, as Jesus commanded a body to be healed, he was channeling the energy of the Holy Spirit within Him, and directing this energy to accomplish a specific purpose, which it did.

Personal Testimony

In the past, confessing a word of faith has not been a strong point for me. For years I had been unsure of God's voice within me and consequently had not wanted to step out in faith with a verbal confession and risk bringing embarrassment to God's name. However, as I have continued to journal and have become more and more confident of God's voice, I have gained greater confidence in confessing the purposes of God before they happen.

One such example occurred on a Sunday morning as I waited on the Lord for guidance for the Sunday service. He spoke through my journal that He was going to heal my co-elder's back that evening in the service. His back had been hurt in a farming mishap. I shared it in the morning with my co-elder, and he received it. In the evening service, after sharing this with the whole body, I invited my co-elder to come forward and encouraged the body to gather around and lay hands on him. As we prayed, he was instantly healed, and all pain and soreness left his back immediately, leaving him strong and healthy again.

This was a short-term period of waiting, but it did require my confessing in faith the purposes of God before the visible evidence was there. God then supernaturally released His power.

Establishing Your Confession through the Will of Your Spirit

Once again, I was amazed to find that my spirit had a "will." I knew that mind, will and emotions were part of the soul, but I didn't know that they were part of the spirit. Look at how the following verses teach that we can make decisions, which is a function of the will, within our hearts, or spirits.

> "Paul **purposed** in the spirit to go to Jerusalem" (Acts 19:20)
> "Let each one do just as he has **purposed** in his **heart"** (II Cor. 9:7)
> "Paul **bound** in the **spirit...**" (Acts 20:22)

When we purpose in our spirits, it is a decision with deep **conviction** and substance. It is not easily changed. When we "decide" in our soul it is more of a **preference**, which is much more open to change.

Remember, we speak out of that which fills the heart (Matt. 12:34). So as we incubate the purposes of God and **purpose in our spirits** to follow them, the visible result will be that we will **speak them forth with deep conviction.** We speak out of that which we have purposed in our hearts. One of the fantastic life-giving commands in the New Testament is to speak only words edifying for the need of the moment (Eph. 4:29). If we purpose in our spirits to do this, we find tremendous life flowing within us as we allow our hearts to incubate and our mouths to speak only the edifying, comforting words of the Holy Spirit, never the destructive, negative whispers of satan.

Setting the Will of Your Spirit to Confess the Vision and Rhema of God

After God had given Abraham rhema and vision and Abraham had filled his inner mind with it, God called him to set his inner will to begin speaking it forth. He changed his name from Abram to Abraham, which means "father of multitudes." Thus, every time Abraham spoke his name, he was **declaring forth in faith the promises of God**. Write out Genesis 17:5.

Now carefully and prayerfully write out Mark 11:22-24.

Prayerfully review what you have written and record the insights you see.

Heart faith involves my speaking forth the rhema and vision of God that I am incubating within my heart, knowing that in the fullness of time God will bring it forth.

In Joshua 6, we see the Israelites giving thanks **before** the walls of Jericho had fallen down. In John 11:41-43, Jesus gave thanks **before** Lazarus rose from the tomb.

In Philippians 4:6-8, we are told to couple **thanksgiving** with our prayers and supplication. In so doing, we make prayer really prayer. Let me illustrate.

If I go to God with my needs and in prayer and supplication dump them at His feet and go away, have I prayed? I think not, because prayer is to be a spiritual encounter with God in which **I speak to Him and He speaks to me through spiritual** communion. As I present my supplications to Him, He speaks to me concerning them. He tells me His purposes and goals in each of them. Thus my prayer is turned into thanksgiving, because God has revealed His purposes concerning the situation. My prayer and supplications have been culminated in thanksgiving. I begin confessing forth what God has spoken to me. "Confession" means to "say the same thing." In this manner, I begin saying the same thing that God has spoken to me in prayer. (The course **Communion with God** by the same author will help you learn to pray this way.)

Resting in Faith During the Interval of Time Between Confessing and Receiving

There is often an interval of waiting between the time God speaks His purposes and the time when He brings them forth. Abraham had to confess his name for a year before the promise was fulfilled. Mark 11:23 promises that if one "believes that what he says is going to happen, it **shall** be granted him."

In Hebrews 3 and 4, we have some of the best teaching in the Bible on uniting faith with rhema during the waiting period and thus being able to live in rest and peace, as you wait upon God to accomplish His purposes. Let's consider it now. Please read thoughtfully and prayerfully Hebrews 3 and 4, recording in the space below the truths you glean concerning uniting rhema with faith and thus coming to rest.

I believe that to enter God's rest (a life of inner, restful peace) one must combine the words spoken by God with the inner heart faith given by God. God's words plus God's faith equals God's rest. This makes us unique in a world full of people who have none of these three. We become a ray of hope in a sea of trouble.

Consider the following:

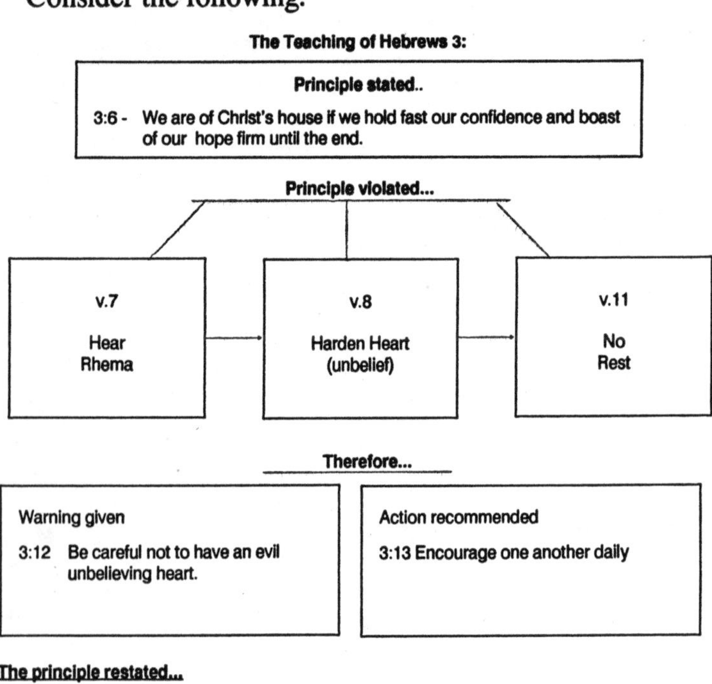

The principle diagrammed..... (3:18,19)

RHEMA + FAITH = REST

RHEMA – FAITH = UNREST

Hebrews 4 Personalized and Summarized

I am created to live in continual rest by uniting faith to the living words of God. I am to confidently confess with my mouth the rhema God has spoken in my heart, calling upon God to give me faith to believe when I am doubting and remembering that Jesus, too, was tempted with doubt and fully understands and relieves my doubts as I call upon Him.

Faith and Patience Inherit the Promises.

As we confess the promises of God, God wants us to wait in patience upon Him to fulfill it. Please write out prayerfully and thoughtfully Hebrews 6:11-15. The reason for writing out Scripture is because the pencil is our best set of eyes. As we write out the Scripture prayerfully, and thoughtfully, God reveals things to us from it which we have never seen before. Therefore, I find writing Scripture one of the best ways to grow in my spiritual life. A space has been provided for you to write these verses.

What is your stated conclusion of these verses?

Encouraged to *Hold on to* Our Confession

"Let us hold fast our confession (Heb. 3:6; 3:14; 4:14)."

"Let us hold fast the confession of our hope without wavering, for He who promised is faithful (Heb. 10:23)."

God would not spend so much time encouraging us to hold fast our confession if it were not going to be a problem for us. We will often be tempted to cease confessing the rhema and vision of God as we wait for His promise to be fulfilled. However, we must know that it will come forth in the fullness of time and that during the interim, God is building patience, perseverance, endurance, steadfastness, and Godly character within us. He may be working brokenness in us, purifying our hearts and motives, and many other things. As we go to Him in communion, He will tell us what He is doing, and what we should be doing, and that will help us stand in patience and faith.

During this time, God wants us to find ways of stimulating one another to love and good deeds. He wants us to assemble together and encourage one another in the faith, and to be careful not to go on sinning, but to heed the word He speaks to us (Heb. 10:24-26).

The Importance of Timing

Notice that it was 24 years after God gave the initial promise to Abraham that He asked him to begin confessing it openly. I believe that this is a critical concept. We do not just begin confessing what God tells us in our own timing and in our own way. God has His perfect timing and His own perfect way for bringing things forth. We must do nothing on our initiative. This includes confessing. We confess when God tells us to confess, and in the way God tells us to confess.

When God places a Divine seed within us in the form of a rhema word or a vision, it is only a seed. It must take root, grow, and become a mighty tree, giving life to those whom it touches. If we confess it too early, and several people scorn that which God has told us He is going to accomplish within and through us, the tender plant may be crushed before it has fully taken root and grown. Therefore, God often has us wait before confessing His rhema and vision. He desires that it become firmly implanted, so that we are able to handle any criticism which may come against us. He has us wait until He has set the stage perfectly for the flow of His Divine action. Then He bids us confess it.

We must be careful, therefore, to listen to God all through the incubation process, so we do not run astray by carrying it out in our own way.

Personal Journaling Application

Lord, is there anything you would like to say to me concerning confessing any of the visions which You have placed within my heart? Record below what He speaks.

Confession Helps Get People Behind God's Ideas.

Another reason for confessing forth the rhema and vision of God is to inspire faith in others and cause them to join with you in establishing the purposes of God. As we learn to share the vision in faith, people become inspired to participate in whatever way God may be asking of them.

However, it is quite a challenge to share the vision in faith, drawing people into it, rather than causing them to react to it. Following are some of the most common obstacles you will encounter, along with some steps to help guide you successfully through them.

Some Common Human Obstacles

1. Many people resist change. Try not to unnecessarily challenge anyone's economic status, self image, or spiritual convictions.
2. There may be the temptation to be over-conforming. Be strong!
3. Criticism may come. Evaluate it and respond only to constructive criticism.
4. Some people may respond with cynicism, envy, or apathy. Keep looking straight ahead at the rhema and vision of God.

Journaling Response

Now look back to the preceding journaling application. Did the Lord ask you to confess any of the visions which He placed within your heart? If so, complete the following.

Lord, of those involved, who are resisting, or who may resist, this proposed change?

Lord, show me if in any way I have challenged their economic status, or self image, or spiritual convictions? If so, how can this be resolved?

Lord, am I weak and over-conforming, properly assertive or rebellious? If I am not properly assertive, what would constitute a proper adjustment?

Lord, speak to me about any criticisms. Show me any constructive ideas which may be in these criticisms. What do you want me to hear from them? How do you want me to respond?

Strategies for Clearing the "People Hurdles"

1. Create in people's minds a need for change by:
   a. making people aware of the problems that currently exist;
   b. warning people about the hazards of not changing; and
   c. stressing the benefits of change FOR THEM.
2. Meet resistance to change with openness and honesty.
3. Involve people in the idea-development process, and listen to their ideas.
4. If possible, implement large changes on a gradual basis.
5. Make tentative changes, trying them out for a period of time.
6. Point out that change and death are the only two certainties in life.

Journaling Response Concerning Strategies for Clearing the "People Hurdles"

Lord, how would you have me create in their minds a need for change?

Lord, show me if I have been open and honest in meeting resistance to change.

Lord, how would you have me involve others in the idea-development process? Have I listened to their ideas?

Lord, are their any gradual stages of implementation (smaller steps) for this vision which you would have me share with the people?

Lord, have I been like Daniel, in that I have presented tentative changes rather than dogmatic declarations? (Dan. 1,2)

Building a Team of Winners

1. Surround yourself with faith-building visionaries, who have their feet on the ground.
2. Recruit the best people available.
3. Let those you've recruited flow in their gifting.
4. Offer your team members goals that are challenging and meaningful to them.
5. Give people the right to disagree.
6. Be lavish in praise and recognition of your team members. (Eph. 4:29-31)

Personal Journaling Concerning Building a Team

Lord, who are the people of faith, who are visionaries, who have their feet on the ground, who ought to be working alongside me?

Lord, are there any people with excellent qualifications in these areas set before me, that You would have me recruit to work alongside me?

Lord, am I letting those whom I've recruited flow freely in the giftings which You have placed within them?

Lord, show me how to offer team members goals that are challenging and meaningful to them.

Lord, am I giving people the right to disagree with me?

Lord, am I being lavish in giving praise and recognition to the team members around me?

Establishing Good Contacts

1. Consider whom you know that might be able to help you.
2. Talk over your ideas with your friends. Discover whom they know who might be able to help you.
3. Start looking for people and organizations that may be able to use your ideas.
4. Talk with strangers you meet.
5. Go where the action is.

Journaling Response

Lord, who are the people I know who may be able to help me?

Lord, with which of my friends should I discuss this idea or vision?

Lord, what organizations may be able to help me in fulfilling this idea or vision?

Record the ideas and contacts you have gotten from strangers with whom you have talked. Then ask the Lord which ones He wants you to key in on.

Lord, what is the best location (i.e., locality, city, region, state) for me to be to accomplish this goal?

Submitting Summarized Findings for Verification

Before we move into Chapter 9, which is "Acting on God's Rhema and Vision," it is time to solidify into a summary and tentative report the vision, goal, and projected steps of action which you have so far.

Take this report to a person who has *proven ability in the area which you are exploring* and present it to him for his recommendation. Be sure to pick a person with proven ability. If your idea involves several areas of expertise, you should present it to people who have proven themselves in each of these areas.

To discover these people, think of those whom you know who have a proven area of expertise in the area in which you are creating. Contact these people to see if they will allow you to submit your proposal to them. Ask them to meet with you to give you their recommendation.

If they have any suggestions, do everything you can to revise your plan for fulfilling your vision, incorporating their suggestions.

It is also recommended that you take your plan to your greatest critic. Present it to him, and ask him to show you any weaknesses he sees in it. Seek to revise your plan, strengthening it in any areas in which he has seen weaknesses.

Obviously, you are being asked to do a lot of work. **However, success demands a lot of work.** If you follow this process through to the end, carrying every step out in completeness and prayer, sensing the intuitive directions of the Lord Jesus Christ, as well as the analytical calculations of your mind, and revising and revising (without stopping mid-pregnancy in frustration), you will give birth to great creative ideas and solutions to problems facing you and your world. Not only will you prosper from it. The world which you serve with your creativity will be blessed, also.

Chapter 9

Filling the Fifth Sense of Man's Spirit by Acting in Faith

Man's Spirit Has Emotions.

Now we come to the fifth faculty of man's spirit, the ability to sense emotions. Once again I was amazed to find that man's spirit had the capacity to feel emotions. I knew one could feel emotions with his soul, but I never realized that the deep underlying emotions that affect my entire behavior and actions flowed from my spirit. Let's observe what the Bible says concerning deep underlying emotions flowing from your heart or spirit.

Ahab's **spirit** was **sullen** because he did not get what he wanted (I Kings 21:5).

Upon hearing Jesus unfold Scripture, the disciples' **hearts burned** within them (Lk. 24:32).

God hardened Ezekiel, sending him embittered in the **rage** of his **spirit** (Ezek. 3:8,14).

In each of these cases, we see that deep underlying

	SENSE	HOW USED	BIBLE EXAMPLE	STAGE
1.	Inner Ear (Jn 5:30)	Receives God's Rhema	Gen 12:1-3	CONCEPTION
2.	Inner Eye (Rev 4:1)	Receives God's Vision	Gen 15:5,6	
3.	Inner Mind (Lk 2:19)	Ponders God's Thoughts	Rom 4:20,21	INCUBATION
4	Inner Will . (Acts 19:21)	Speaks on God's Rhema	Gen 17:5	
5.	**Inner Emotions (1 King 21:5)**	**Acts on God's Rhema And Vision**	**Gen 17:23**	
	END RESULT	Death of the Vision "I" am unable to Bring it about	Gen 16:2 Gen 17:18,19	BIRTH
		Supernatural resurrection of the Vision. "In the fullness of Time GOD brings it forth."	Gen 21:1,2 Gal 4:4a	

emotions are being felt in man's spirit, rather than man's soul. There are many other verses which talk of deep underlying emotions centered in man's heart or spirit. Here are some of them for your reference.

Gen. 41:8; Ps. 142:3; Dan. 7:15; Ex. 6:9; Prov. 15:13; Jn. 11:33; I Sam. 1:15; Eccl. 10:4; Acts 17:16; Job 21:4; Isa. 19:3; Gen. 45:26; Ps. 34:18; Isa. 54:6

From these scriptures, we see that many deep emotions flow from man's spirit. Watchman Nee says that "emotions are the channel of the Spirit." In other words, deep underlying emotions are the avenue by which the Holy Spirit flows out through us. This concept totally reversed my theology and practice. Previous to understanding this, I had largely cut off my emotions as being soulish and not valid in Christian ministry. Now I see them (emotions of the spirit; not emotions of the soul) as being valid and vital and needful of cultivation.

Once again the general rule for dividing soul from spirit is this: "That which comes from the soul is external, changeable, and reactionary; that which comes from the spirit has substance, is deep and underlying." I believe Paul divides asunder the emotions of the soul from the emotions of the spirit in II Cor. 4:8 when he says "perplexed but not despairing." Paul's soul was perplexed but his spirit would not despair. Both of these are emotions. Paul says in verse 6, that the light of Jesus shining within his heart would not allow his heart to despair even though his soul was perplexed at the circumstances around him.

Both our souls and our spirits feel emotions. The deep consuming emotions of our spirits are what motivate us to action. Until the emotions of our heart are touched, we will not act. For instance, we may know that there are starving children all around the world, but that knowledge will not move us to action. However, once the deep wellsprings of compassion within our hearts have been touched in regard to this situation, we will find ourselves moved to action. Emotions are the wellsprings of action.

Now, one final point. Not only do our actions flow from thc deep underlying emotions of our spirits, but emotions are stimulated by vision. Pictures move us much more deeply than words. A picture touches the emotions of the heart much more adequately than cognitive thoughts. I venture to say that every great speaker who has touched your heart and moved your inner emotions has been a vivid storyteller, one who has painted pictures and drawn you into them.

Our emotions are extremely responsive to vision. Therefore, as you hold the vision of God before your heart, your heart's emotions get excited at what they see, and emotion then leads the way to action.

Actions Flowing from the Emotions and Visions of God.

Now let's turn to Abraham. God **appeared** again to Abram at 99 years of age. The rhema He spoke was couched in vision. God gave specific instruction concerning circumcision. If Abraham had not been incubating the promises and visions of God, I question whether he would have even acted on this most recent, and apparently bizarre, command. However, I'm sure God's fresh appearance, and His freshly spoken word, deeply stirred Abraham's heart, moving him to action. This obedient action brought the Lord's appearance again, with the promise of a son within the year.

Faith must always lead to action. Peter's faith caused him to walk on water. The ten lepers were told to **go** and in going they were healed. Rahab, the harlot, hid the two spies. James says that faith without works is dead (James 2:22,26).

Often the action of faith may be illogical to the natural senses. Some examples are: the Israelites walking around the walls of Jericho; Naaman going to dip seven times in the Jordan to be healed of leprosy; the blind man being told to wash in the pool of Siloam; and the ten lepers who were told to go show themselves to the priest for inspection while they still had leprosy. These "illogical" acts of faith brought forth the supernatural provisions of the Lord.

Whatever the Lord is asking of you as an act of faith, it is wise to fulfill it so that the supernatural provision of God can be released.

A Personal Example

Let me share one time when I felt very "foolish" in having to act on the vision God had given me.

I had just finished leading a stranger to the Lord. I had stressed total lordship and true repentance, so that he would not be presumably saved through "a cheap Gospel." I made certain he understood that he must lay his life down for Christ, and that through losing his life he would find it. He prayed a sincere repentance and committal of his life to the Lord. As we sat quietly in my study at the close of the prayer, I felt good. I felt that this man was soundly converted. As he still had his head bowed, I decided to present my inner eye to Jesus to see if He had anything He wanted to show me. A vision appeared of the Holy Spirit surrounding the man, but not able to enter because of turmoil going on within him. I was startled and wanted to reject the vision because I did not think it could be true. I felt confident in my mind that this man had just been saved. Thus, how could the Holy Spirit be still outside him and not have entered his heart?

I opened my eyes and asked if he felt that anything had happened, because I believe that when one is saved, the Holy Spirit bears witness with his spirit that he is a child of God. If the Holy Spirit is not bearing witness within, who am I to tell from without that the Holy Ghost has moved? Therefore, I believe a newly saved person will feel something, not in his soulish emotions, but in the emotions of his spirit.

The man looked up and said, "I don't think anything happened." I was dumbstruck. This blew away my theology. According to everything I'd learned, this man should have been saved, and he should have known it in his spirit. However, his confession lined up with my "bizarre" vision. So I said to him, "I don't think anything happened either." Then the Lord revealed that the man was harboring an immoral love relationship and planning to divorce his wife in favor of a younger woman. I told him that in choosing Christ as Lord, he would have to give up this love relationship and commit himself to his wife. He said he was unwilling to do this. I responded that Christ then could not be his Lord, and salvation would not be his until he was willing to lay down his life and follow after Christ.

God's vision may call us to "bizarre" conclusions. Yet, when we act upon them, God will disclose His supernatural truth.

Personal Study of Hebrews 11 — The Faith Chapter

Read Hebrews 11, the Faith Chapter at least four times, slowly, thoughtfully and prayerfully, recording the following:

1. In the first reading, note and record the acts that **faith** accomplished.

2. In the second reading, note and record the truths concerning dying in faith without receiving the promises of God.

3. In the third reading, note and record the world's view of these men and God's view of them.

4. In the fourth reading, record any other insights God gives you as you read prayerfully, waiting for revelation. What is God saying to you as you move into this realm of acting upon heart faith?

Prayer: "Lord, we have been fools for the world long enough. Now may You make us willing to become 'fools' for You."

On the following page you will find an overview diagram of the process of carrying a dream or vision from inception to completion. It is laid out by **The Lead Group, Inc.** and is added to give you another pictorial overview of the entire process of long range planning, or birthing a vision from God. On a separate sheet of paper, you may want to work through the steps of this diagram with a project which God has placed in front of you. Use journaling at each stage of the process. In that way, you will have God's ideas, rather than just yours.

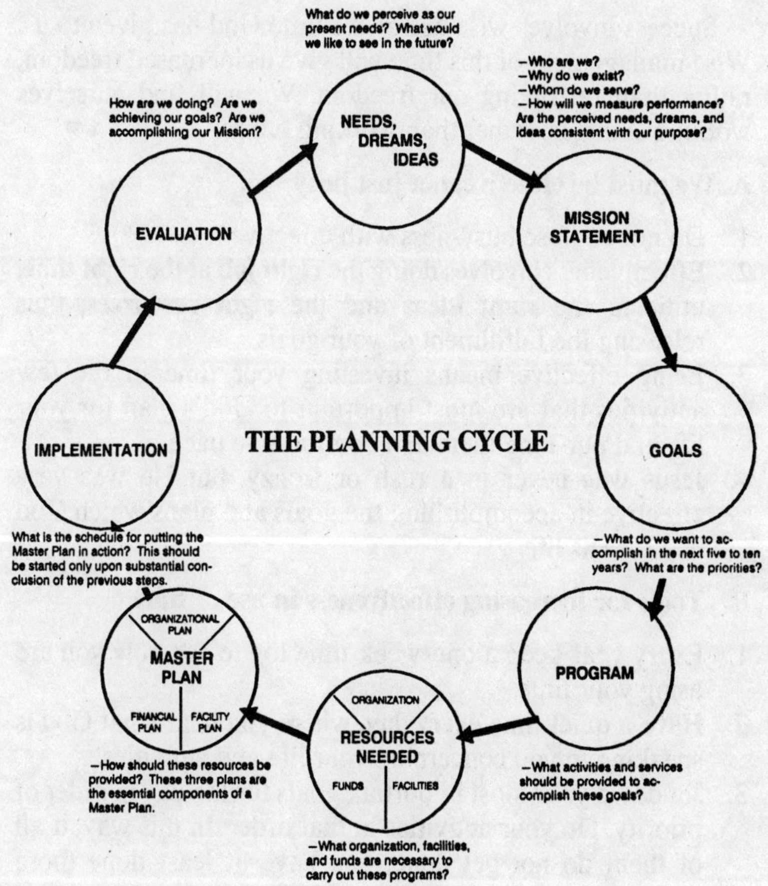
Long Range Planning
THE PLANNING CYCLE
What do we perceive as our present needs? What would we like to see in the future?
NEEDS, DREAMS, IDEAS
–Who are we?
–Why do we exist?
–Whom do we serve?
–How will we measure performance?
Are the perceived needs, dreams, and ideas consistent with our purpose?
MISSION STATEMENT
GOALS
–What do we want to accomplish in the next five to ten years? What are the priorities?
PROGRAM
–What activities and services should be provided to accomplish these goals?
ORGANIZATION
RESOURCES NEEDED
FUNDS
FACILITIES
–What organization, facilities, and funds are necessary to carry out these programs?
ORGANIZATIONAL PLAN
MASTER PLAN
FINANCIAL PLAN
FACILITY PLAN
–How should these resources be provided? These three plans are the essential components of a Master Plan.
What is the schedule for putting the Master Plan in action? This should be started only upon substantial conclusion of the previous steps.
IMPLEMENTATION
EVALUATION
How are we doing? Are we achieving our goals? Are we accomplishing our Mission?

Investing Time Wisely

Success involves wise use of the time God has given to us. Wise management of this time will give us increased freedom, rather than restricting our freedom. We will find ourselves working **smarter**, rather than working **harder**.

A. We must be effective, not just busy.

1. Do not confuse busy-ness with effectiveness.
2. Effectiveness involves doing the **right job** at the **right time**, utilizing the **right ideas** and the **right resources**, thus releasing the fulfillment of your goals.
3. Being effective means investing your time in the few activities that are most important to God's plan for your life and pursuing them at a comfortable pace.
4. Jesus was never in a rush or frenzy, but He was very effective in accomplishing the goals and plans which God had for His life.

B. Tools for increasing effectiveness in use of time

1. Every year keep a one-week time log to see how you are using your time.
2. Have a quiet time every day, where you hear what God is speaking to you concerning your life and activities.
3. Jot down your most important goals for the day in order of priority. Do your activities in that order. In this way, if all of them do not get done, you have at least done those which were most important.
4. Match up each job with the time of day when you are most effective in accomplishing that type of activity.
5. Keep your schedule loose so that God, people, and problems can break in upon it, as they most certainly will.
6. Schedule times of relaxation so your heart can incubate the things God is generating within you.

7. Look for ways to effectively use time slots in your day that are not now being used effectively.

C. Minimizing interruptions and distractions

1. Ask: "Is this urgent, or is it important, or is it both?" Realize that often the urgent is not that important.
2. Say **NO** to those things that you sense are not God's call upon your time for this period of your life.
   The following things are better left undone:
   a. all low priority items;
   b. any task whose completion is of little or no consequence:
   c. anything you can give to someone else to do;
   d. anything you do just to please others because you fear their condemnation or desire their approval;
   e. thoughtless or inappropriate requests for your time or effort;
   f. anything others should be doing for themselves.
3. If you work in an office use techniques to minimize drop-in visits.
   a. Close the door when you're doing work that requires solitude.
   b. Remove excess chairs and social amenities from your office or work area.
   c. If someone wants to see you, go to his place to talk.
   d. If you are constantly interrupted by subordinates wanting help with problems, have them write down the problem and three possible solutions, in order of priority.
   e. Use body language.
   f. Arrange your desk so it faces away from the door.
   g. Have your secretary screen your visitors.
   h. Use lunch hours and coffee breaks to meet with necessary visitors.

4. Use techniques to minimize telephone calls.
   a. Use the telephone instead of writing letters and memos.
   b. Group your calls and place them during the morning.
   c. Try to limit most calls to three minutes.
   d. When possible have an assistant screen your calls.
   e. Outline the material you want to cover before you place the call.
5. Hide away when you need uninterrupted blocks of time. Go to a separate room, a library, another office, a hotel room, your car.
6. Batch your trivia work and do it at one time.

D. Can you cut back on either of these?

1. The amount of time you spend sleeping

2. The amount of time you spend watching TV

Personal Journaling Application

1. Lord, am I just keeping busy, rather than being effective? Are there any alterations in my life and work which You would like me to make to help move me from busy-ness to effectiveness?

2. Lord, is there any way in which I can better match the types of jobs I do with various time slots in my day?

3. Lord, am I scheduling adequate and appropriate relaxation times for myself and my family?

4. Lord, am I being moved by that which is important, or driven by that which is urgent?

5. Lord, am I leaving undone those things which I am not supposed to be doing?

6. Lord, am I handling drop in visits and telephones calls properly?

7. Lord, am I spending the proper amount of time sleeping and watching television?

Stage Three - Birth of Miracle

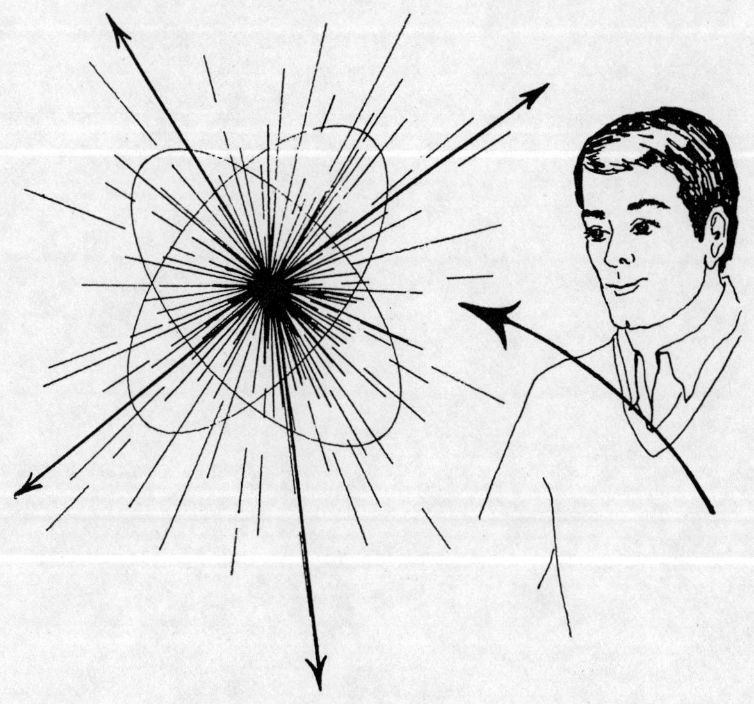

"In the Fullness of Time, God brought forth. . ." (Gal. 4:4)

Chapter 10

Death and Resurrection of the Vision

Introduction — The Process Reviewed

Finally, we come near the end of the development of heart faith. But before we actually receive the promise of God, we often go through the experience of death of a vision. However, before exploring this, let's review the process.

We began with a word and a vision placed within our hearts by God. These things we incubated within. We filled our inner mind, will and emotions with God's word and vision. We pondered them, allowing them to go round and round, letting them grow until, just like a baby, they were delivered forth in the fullness of time. As Dr. Cho says, whatever is incubated in the fourth dimension is created in the third dimension. Or in other words, when we incubate the vision and rhema of God within our spirits, we will find them delivered forth into the world in which we live.

Thus, by incubating the creative words and visions of God, we too can become creative. We become like Jesus, our

	SENSE	HOW USED	BIBLE EXAMPLE	STAGE
1.	Inner Ear (Jn 5:30)	Receives God's Rhema	Gen 12:1-3	CONCEPTION
2.	Inner Eye (Rev 4:1)	Receives God's Vision	Gen 15:5,6	
3.	Inner Mind (Lk 2:19)	Ponders God's Thoughts	Rom 4:20,21	INCUBATION
4	Inner Will (Acts 19:21)	Speaks on God's Rhema	Gen 17:5	
5.	Inner Emotions (1 Kings 21:5)	Acts on God's Rhema And Vision	Gen 17:23	
	END RESULT	**Death of the Vision "I" am unable to Bring it about**	**Gen 16:2** **Gen 17:18,19**	**BIRTH**
		Supernatural resurrection of the Vision. "In the fullness of Time GOD brings it forth."	Gen 21:1,2 Gal 4:4a	

perfect example. He spoke only the words He heard from the Father and did only the things He saw the Father doing, thereby becoming a channel of creative power bringing healing, deliverance, and Godly wisdom into the situations around Him. I am convinced that as we follow His example of living and speaking only out of the Father's voice and vision, we too will live and move as Jesus did.

Death of the Vision — Illustrated in Abraham's Life

There is one very painful experience that we generally walk through before this all becomes reality within our lives. That is death and resurrection, or, the "death of a vision."

Let's look at Abraham. He **did** receive the promise of faith that he had incubated for **twenty-five** years. Please write out Genesis 21:5.

However, Abraham had experienced what we will call "death of a vision." In the ways of God, we find that He consistently takes us through a three-step process: (1) birth of a vision, (2) death of a vision, and (3) supernatural fulfillment of the vision.

God gives birth to the vision by granting it initially to us. However, we generally try to fulfill that vision under our own strength, thus enabling us to share in its glory. But all glory is to go to God. God has not granted us a natural religion which we can fulfill in our own strength. Christianity ascends far above creed and ethics into the supernatural manifestation of God.

Notice how in Abram's and Sarai's impatience with the timing of God, they sought to fulfill the vision through their own means (Gen. 16), and gave birth to Ishmael through Sarai's maid. Thirteen years later, Abraham was still hoping that his method was acceptable to God (Gen. 17:18,19): "Oh that Ishmael might live before Thee!" But God said "No." By this time Abram was ninety-nine years old. There was no longer any way in the natural that the vision could be fulfilled. The vision had died and Abram had to die to self. There was nothing more he could do, except wait upon God and be obedient to Him. And that he did. God spoke again, giving more specific commands which Abraham **immediately** carried out, causing God to speak to him again, promising him a child supernaturally within the year (Gen. 17,18). Isaac was born within that year.

After the death of a vision comes the supernatural fulfillment of the vision, **if we will continue to seek God and obey Him during this period of darkness.**

Not only did Abraham have to die to this vision once, but a second time God called him to offer up the vision. God asked Abraham to sacrifice Isaac on the altar. By this time, Abraham had grown wise in the ways of God. He knew that as the vision died again within him, God could and would bring supernatural fulfillment out of it. Write out Abraham's thoughts as recorded in Hebrews 11:19.

God will ask us to give up the vision over and over, so that we know that it is His and not ours, Him and not us, that He may be glorified in all things.

The Teaching and Example of Jesus

Prayerfully and meditatively write out John 12:23b-25a. What do these verses say to you?

The principle of all of life is that resurrection life flows out of death. A seed is resurrected into a tree after it dies. Jesus was resurrected into glory after He died. God's rhema and visions will be supernaturally resurrected after they have died to the flesh.

Jesus told His disciples that He was going to usher in "the Kingdom." That vision and rhema word died in their hearts as Jesus hung on the cross, only to be supernaturally fulfilled a few days later at Pentecost, as God fulfilled the vision and rhema word in a way far exceeding their expectations.

Other Scriptural Examples of Death of a Vision

Joseph in his youth was given a vision of ruling over his brothers and parents. That vision died to any natural fulfillment as Joseph was sold into slavery and put into prison. Through these hardships, God worked, perfecting humility and brokenness so that in the fullness of time God could supernaturally resurrect the vision. Now, however, God could place a meek, humble man in leadership, rather than an arrogant unbroken youth. **God is always working His purposes, even through the death of a vision.**

Moses was commissioned to free the Israelites from Egyptian bondage. So, in the flesh, he went out and slew the first Egyptian he saw harassing an Israelite. God had to lead him to the backside of the wilderness for forty years where He matured Moses and taught him His ways. Then God supernaturally fulfilled the vision.

These are a few of the examples of death of a vision in Scripture. You will find others as you study.

How to Triumphantly Pass through Death

No one wants to experience death. It is a painful, undesired experience. Many Christians will not embrace the cross, not discerning the purposes of God nor seeing the resurrection glory that God desires to bring forth on the other side of it. Therefore, many Christians never pass into supernatural Christianity, but stay on the safer, less painful and less fulfilling side of the cross. Jesus triumphantly endured the cross. Write out Hebrews 12:2, noting how He did it.

Jesus did not fix His eyes on the cross. Yes, He had to go through with it, and yes, it would be painful. However, there is no life in clinging to the cross.

One gains the strength he needs to pass through the cross by looking at the joy set before him.

My eyes must be fixed on the purposes of God that are going to be supernaturally resurrected out of the death experience. Jesus saw through Calvary to resurrection glory and this vision and joy gave Him the strength to endure the cross.

"For the joy set before Him, endured the cross" — Heb. 12:2

One is tempted to fix his eyes on the hardship of the cross as he is passing through death. If one does so, he is liable to falter and fail. Jesus went to Gethesemane and prayed in agony, fixing His eyes on the purpose and strength of God. The ordeal was won in agonizing prayer. God's purposes were strengthened deep within Jesus' heart, and grace was given to endure the suffering.

We, too, must win the battle in agonizing prayer. As we cry out to God over and over, we find strength and vision being re-established deep within our hearts.

THIS IS WHERE THE BATTLE IS EITHER WON OR LOST. THIS IS WHERE ONE EITHER ENTERS OR FAILS TO ENTER SUPERNATURAL CHRISTIANITY.

Gethsemane prepares us for Calvary. Calvary prepares us for Glory.

Some may object and say that Christ suffered so we would not need to suffer. No, Christ suffered so that our suffering could be united with His suffering and that, being intertwined, God's grace would be allowed to flow.

Suffering Death in the Flesh and Ceasing from Sin

Part of what is fulfilled in death of a vision is the death of self and sin within my flesh, resulting in my becoming more alive to the righteousness of Christ. Please write out I Peter 4:1,13.

Clearly we are told that suffering is part of our lot, and that good can come out of it, if we keep our eyes focused on Christ while we walk through it (I Pet. 4:12-19). Therefore, it is important for us to discern the purposes of God. We need to be in communion, especially as we pass through the death of a vision. In communion, we find understanding and strength to help us endure. With the understanding comes the opportunity for us to cooperate with God in His glorious workings. Rather than running from death, we can embrace it with understanding, cooperation and strength, being transformed from glory to glory while we look not at the things seen, but at the things unseen. Then we enter into supernatural Christianity.

Supernatural Fulfillment of the Vision

We have covered this aspect partially in the earlier chapters. Genesis 17 and 18 contain principles that lay the groundwork for the supernatural fulfillment of the vision. Communion is re-established in Abram's life after a 13 year break. God's first words to him were a call to total obedience.

"Walk before me and be blameless (Gen. 17:1)." God was looking for holiness. He did not reject Abram because he had failed miserably in self-effort. However, He did require holiness before final fulfillment of the covenant. In Genesis 17:23, we see that Abraham obeyed God's specific commands "in the very same day" that they were given. This opened the way for God to commune more with Abraham (Gen. 18:1). In this further communion, God for the first time set a date for the culmination of the vision, within the year.

I have found that prayer, fasting, communion and obedience pave the way for the supernatural fulfillment of God. **Every major move in my spiritual life has flowed out of prayer, fasting, communion and obedience.**

Personal Illustration

May I give an illustration from Dr. Cho's life.

Dr. Cho had burning within his heart a vision of having the largest church in Korea. As he strove to fulfill that vision in the flesh, he came to the point of total exhaustion which was so complete that for a long period of time he was not even able to carry out his responsibilities as pastor. Thus, he entered the death process, and all personal ambition died, along with the vision for the largest church in Korea. However, God was at work, perfecting the vessel, breaking the ambitious pride and molding a meek individual. God told Dr. Cho it would be ten years before his body was completely healed, because God knew it would take ten years to perfect the qualities of characters that He was building through the suffering Dr. Cho was experiencing.

During those ten years, God built a cellular structure within Dr. Cho's church which allowed him to far surpass any dream or vision previously given. He not only has the largest church in Korea, but also the largest church in the world. So such things happen in our lives as we understand and cooperate with the ways of God and enter into spiritual communion with Him, faithfully carrying out His commands to us.

Personal Journaling Application

Ask God to show you where you are in this whole process. Record what He tells you.

Prayer: "Lord, may we live in the vision of resurrection Glory!"

Quickly Passing through the Desert Experience of Death

Some people live continually in death. They are always suffering for Jesus. They are always going through some horrendous thing. They just never seem to get to the promised land. And they think that this is what God wishes, desires and plans for them. Well, I have news for them: We are to pass through our deserts as quickly as possible and move on into the promised land of Canaan!

The Israelites could have crossed the desert in 12 days, yet they took 40 years. The generation that left Egypt had to die in the desert. We do not have to continue to make circles around Mount Sinai. We can learn to move quickly and cooperatively with the purposes of God, and learn to live in the promised land of life, rather than the desert of death. Therefore, it is important that we learn to clearly see, and understand, and effectively handle situational hurdles that appear in our lives. The following outlines some common hurdles and allows you the opportunity of journaling your way through them. The purpose of this exercise is to help you move as quickly as possible through the tough spots, and into the promised land that flows with milk and honey.

Clearing Situational Hurdles Which Could Prevent the Fulfillment of a Vision

A. The following appear to be situational hurdles; however, in reality, they are not.

1. IMPATIENCE — Make sure you are not expecting too much too soon. The greater the success you seek, the more time it's likely to take.
2. POORLY DEFINED GOALS — Do you have well delineated goals, that were birthed in prayer? Has God given you a plan that makes every day count? Are these

goals specific, measurable and accompanied with target dates? Are you caught in the activity trap?

3. DISORGANIZATION — Do you have an overall sense of direction and commitment? Good organization means choosing a proper work environment, getting the proper training and tools to do the job and arranging things in a way that will enable you to be comfortable and have easy access to the tools you need.
4. FEELING THAT YOU FACE AN OVERWHELMING PROBLEM OR GOAL — Break large projects down into numerous minor tasks and tackle them one at a time. "Inch by inch, anything's a cinch."

B. Clearing the real situational hurdles

1. DIVINE PROVIDENCE — In order to more effectively flow with the purposes of God in life consider the following:
   a. There is a Divine timing for everything. "In the fullness of time God brought forth...." Be prepared to sense and cooperate with the timing of the Lord.
   b. Be open to God showing you things by "accident" that you were not even looking for.
   c. Remember that God's grace flows FROM ONE TO ANOTHER. Cultivate new friendships.
   d. ACT creatively to assist in the realization of your goals.
   e. Listen closely to the intuitive voice of the Holy Spirit within you.
   f. Be willing to step out in faith.
   g. Move prayerfully and quickly to minimize your losses.
   h. Ask the Lord to give you a backup plan, just in case things do not go as planned. God had a backup plan for this universe, and when man sinned, it went into action.

i. Don't assume that life owes you. You are to give yourself to life.

2. MONEY — Just because you don't have money doesn't mean you can't get the capital you need to start your idea on its way to realization. Good ideas attract money.
   a. Borrow money when necessary for business enterprises.
   b. Raise money by selling off tangible assets.
   c. Seek a creative idea for raising money.
   d. Consider taking a second job.
3. INEXPERIENCE — Everyone starts with inexperience and gains experience. Internally one needs to be willing to make mistakes as he learns. One can gain external experience through the following.
   a. Volunteer to work for someone at no pay for the privilege of learning and gaining experience.
   b. Credentials can compensate somewhat for a lack of experience.
   c. Radiate self-confidence, enthusiasm, and a willingness to learn.
   d. Act in faith externally that which you desire and see internally, thus freeing the way for its creation.

Clearing Situational Hurdles — Personal Application

REMEMBER: Keep your eyes fixed on Jesus as you pray and present these questions before **HIM.** Watch what **HE** speaks and does concerning them.

1. IMPATIENCE — Lord, am I expecting too much too soon? Speak to me concerning how You see the situation.

2. GOALS — Lord, please remind me of the goals that you have placed within my heart. What are the long range goals? What am I to be doing at this time?

3. DISORGANIZATION — Lord, do I have the proper work environment, training and tools to do the job you are asking me to do? Is there anything You want to add at this time?

4. FEELING THAT YOU FACE AN OVERWHELMING PROBLEM OR GOAL — Lord, is there any way you want me to break down this task that I am not seeing at this time? Show me how You want me to progress, a piece at a time.

5. SYNCHRONIZING YOUR ACTIVITIES WITH GOD'S TIMING —
   a. Lord, am I in Your perfect timing in what I am doing at this time?

b. Is there anything that You're trying to show me that I am not seeing?

c. Are there new friends that You want to introduce me to? Who are they? How will I discover them?

d. Lord, is there any action that You want me to carry out at this time which I am not currently doing?

e. Lord, is there any backup plan that You want to give me? If so, what is it?

f. Lord, is my attitude right? Do I think that life owes me, or am I ready to give myself unselfishly as a servant to others?

6. MONEY — Lord, how do You want to provide the money for this venture? Do You want me to borrow it, sell off some items, take a second job, or do You have some other creative idea for releasing the money for this project?

7. INEXPERIENCE — Lord, is there any area where I am lacking in experience in successfully accomplishing this venture? If so, please show me.

   a. Lord, do You want me to gain or use any credentials in accomplishing this goal?

b. Lord, do You want me to volunteer to work for someone to gain some experience in the areas set before me? If so, who? And when?

c. Lord, am I radiating the self-confidence, enthusiasm, and willingness to learn that your Spirit within radiates?

d. Lord, am I acting in faith concerning those things which You have put within my heart?

Chapter 11

Birthing the Rhema and Vision of Almighty God

Thy Kingdom Come, Thy Will be Done on Earth...

Now we have it. The purposes of God, born through the spirit of man. The God of this universe, incarnate in His creation, fulfilling His purposes. Eden restored.

It's what the Prophets spoke about. It's what Jesus demonstrated. It's what the world so desperately needs. It's the fulfillment of God's heart desire. It's the shining light of the glory of God revealed in the heart of man. It's the kingdom of God present and pulsating among us. It's Christianity operating as it should.

Jesus said that when the people saw the supernatural movement of God among them, (healing the sick, casting out of demons, etc.) the kingdom of God was at hand. It was among them. He taught His disciples to pray "Thy kingdom come, Thy will be done, in earth as it is in heaven." This was not a request in the Greek language. It was in the imperative, meaning it was a command!

	SENSE	HOW USED	BIBLE EXAMPLE	STAGE
1.	Inner Ear (Jn 5:30)	Receives God's Rhema	Gen 12:1-3	CONCEPTION
2.	Inner Eye (Rev 4:1)	Receives God's Vision	Gen 15:5,6	
3.	Inner Mind (Lk 2:19)	Ponders God's Thoughts	Rom 4:20,21	INCUBATION
4	Inner Will (Acts 19:21)	Speaks on God's Rhema	Gen 17:5	
5.	Inner Emotions (1 Kings 21:5)	Acts on God's Rhema And Vision	Gen 17:23	
	END RESULT	Death of the Vision "I" am unable to Bring it about	Gen 16:2 Gen 17:18,19	BIRTH
		Supernatural resurrection of the Vision. "In the fullness of Time	**Gen 21:1,2** **Gal 4:4a**	

So now we are to learn to command forth that which we see by vision in the heavenlies, and see it released in the earth in which we live. That is what Jesus did. That is what He commanded His followers to do. That is what they did. That is what we are to do. And now we can. We have learned the principles of heart faith, or Spirit-born creativity, and now we are ready to use them in every area of our lives at all times.

Now we are prepared to be the head and not the tail, the lender and not the borrower, the fruitful, and not the cursed. We have learned to flow in the supernatural power of Almighty God. Now there are no limits to our lives. Only God. And there are very few limits in God. The Lord has spoken over and over to me saying, "Mark, now there are no limits in your life. You have now entered into My limitlessness. My vastness. My Power. My ability. There are now no limits in your life."

How exciting! No longer am I limited by my own ability, my background, my weaknesses. I can now enter into the vastness of God. What a privilege! What a joy! What an honor! Glory to His name.

Now you, too, can enter into the limitlessness and vastness of Almighty God. Now you, too, have no limits in your life. Only the limits of Almighty God. Now you, too, are given power and vastness far beyond your own physical frame. You have entered into the world of Holy Spirit-born creativity. You have learned to birth the purposes of God. You have been restored as a ruler and authority, seated with Christ in heavenly places at the right hand of God.

Birthing Takes Effort

At the time of delivery, all your energies will be required. You must give yourself totally to that which is at hand. It is hard work to actually deliver the baby which God has placed within you. Therefore, expect there to be periods of such times in your life. Realize that they are only periods. They do not last forever. However, you must give your total attention to them during the period in which they are being birthed.

A Personal Example

During 1987, the Lord began speaking to me about doing desktop publishing and offset printing in-house. We were spending many thousands of dollars each month on our printing bill, and it seemed that it could be cut drastically if we did our own work. After three or four months of journaling and researching, (which the Lord told me to do in my journal), we made the decision to go in-house with our printing. I thought, "Now the work is finished." Was I in for a surprise! You see, I was placed in charge of the desk-top publishing and off-set printing, and I knew nothing about either. I was responsible for getting both systems up and going, seeing that volunteers were trained and placed on the equipment and that work flowed smoothly and evenly from one department to another. In addition, I had to keep sufficient inventory on the shelves of approximately 100 items which we sold to thousands of customers. To birth this took me the entire summer. It caused much stretching and growing, since I knew absolutely nothing about desktop publishing or offset printing. I needed to give my entire attention to it. The Lord instructed me to give my entire attention to it, not to give it a lick and a promise, but to see that it was all set up right. By the time fall arrived, all was running smoothly, and I was able to turn part of my attention to other things.

So you see, there will be times in your life when you are actually giving birth to the movement and plan of God, and during those times you will have to give your total attention to that which you are doing. Realize that it is only a temporary situation. You will go back to times of rest, before you are called upon to birth something new.

Personal Journaling Application

Describe a time in your life when God has had you in the midst of the birthing process. Are you now in the midst of birthing any of the visions which God has placed within your heart? If so describe the situation.

Prayer: Thank you Lord, that You have chosen to birth Your kingdom through mankind, through your chosen servants.

Chapter 12

Giving All The Glory To God

So now we have it. The birthing process is complete. The job is done. Everyone is excited. (Ecstatic is more like it!) Everyone is congratulating each other. What a wonderful thing we have accomplished.

How do we handle the glory that comes our way when we are used mightily to fulfill the purposes of God? It makes **us** look good to be around at times like these. However, you and I know that it wasn't our power that accomplished this miracle. Nor was it our idea. We were not the ones who set everything in motion and perfectly timed all the moving parts. We were just caught in the flow of Almighty God. What a joy to be caught in His flow!

Now what do we do when people come up and congratulate us? First of all, **we know** with conviction that it is God within us they are appreciating, and we are so conscious of this that we simply translate all this glory and praise inwardly by smiling and saying, "Thank you, Jesus. It is great to flow with You and be a blessing to others." Outwardly we may say, "I'm glad it was a blessing to you," or, "Praise God. God is truly

	SENSE	HOW USED	BIBLE EXAMPLE	STAGE
1.	Inner Ear (Jn 5:30)	Receives God's Rhema	Gen 12:1-3	CONCEPTION
2.	Inner Eye (Rev 4:1)	Receives God's Vision	Gen 15:5,6	
3.	Inner Mind (Lk 2:19)	Ponders God's Thoughts	Rom 4:20,21	INCUBATION
4	Inner Will (Acts 19:21)	Speaks on God's Rhema	Gen 17:5	
5.	Inner Emotions (1 Kings 21:5)	Acts on God's Rhema And Vision	Gen 17:23	
	END RESULT	Death of the Vision "I" am unable to Bring it about	Gen 16:2 Gen 17:18,19	BIRTH
		Supernatural resurrection of the Vision. "In the fullness of Time GOD brings it forth."	Gen 21:1,2 Gal 4:4a	

awesome, isn't He?" We laugh and join in the joy and ecstasy of what God has done through us, because we are so conscious that it was God.

We know that we know that we know that He is the Alpha and the Omega, the Beginning and the End, and that besides Him there is no other. Our self-confidence and self reliance has been broken because He has taken us through death of a vision. We know that we stand *only* because of His grace. We are totally conscious of our weakness and His power. Life is our weakness being joined to His strength. Our lives have been hidden in Him. So we can even say, "Thank you" when a person compliments us, knowing that it is Jesus who is saying, "Thank you."

Don't We Need to Fear Pride Creeping into Our Lives?

I don't think so. If we fear and reverence God, and commune with Him, He takes care of the rest. I find as I journal, He reminds me of who He is and who I am. If I start to become too cocky, thinking I can handle things, He asks me to kneel when I pray or worship, reminding me of our relationship. He may allow my weaknesses to surface, driving me once again into His arms for mercy and strength. Yes, He has many ways of keeping me humble and meek before Him and before my brothers.

I think it is only the person who fails to commune who can go off on a tangent of pride and arrogance. Therefore, I encourage you to continue to journal, and you will find that God will keep your pride in check. If you fail to commune, then yes, I think you need to fear pride creeping into your life and destroying you.

Being Relaxed, Laughing, and Enjoying Life

We must keep an attitude of play as we walk through life. Don't take yourself too seriously. Take God seriously. See Him as the moving agent in all of life. See yourself as someone who becomes caught in His flow and carried along. Laugh and enjoy His majesty and beauty. Enjoy the life of communion He has given you. Enjoy the unbelievable creativity that flows through you. Realize that as long as you keep laughing and not taking yourself too seriously, He can do great things through you.

May God be radiated in the life you live. Peace!

Personal Journaling Application

Lord, am I giving all the glory for everything in my life to You? Please speak to me about this.

APPENDICES

APPENDIX A. Understanding the Power of Rhema: "The Spoken Word"

APPENDIX B. Allowing God to Restore Your Visionary Capacity

APPENDIX C. Summary Diagram of Death of a Vision

APPENDIX D. Other Lessons Abraham Learned in His Walk of Faith

Appendix A

Understanding The Power of Rhema: "The Spoken Word"

	Kind of Rhema	Biblical Examples
Most life-giving	I speak that which God is currently speaking within. (i.e. my rhema comes forth from His rhema).	". . . The words (rhema) that I say . . . I do not speak on my own initiative, but the Father abiding in Me does His works (Jn. 14:10)." ". . . The words (rhema) which Thou gavest me I have given to them . . . (Jn. 17:8)." (See also Lk. 1:38; 5:5; Jn. 5:19, 20, 30; 8:26, 28, 38; 3:34; 6:63; Acts 10:13, II Cor. 12:4; Eph. 6:17; Heb. 11:3; 12:19).
Somewhat life-giving	I speak the written Word of God.	". . . Stand and continue to speak to the people in the temple the whole message (rhema) of this life (Acts 5:20)."
Neutral	I speak out of myself.	". . . By the mouth of two or three witnesses every word (rhema) may be confirmed (Matt. 18:16)."
Somewhat destructive	I speak the generalized word of satan, which I have heard in the past.	". . . Every evil word (rhema) that men shall speak, they shall render account for it in the day of judgement (Matt. 13:36)."
Most destructive	I speak that which satan is currently speaking within.	". . . We have heard him speak blasphemous words (rhema) against . . . God (Acts 6:11)." "The tongue is a fire . . . set on fire by hell (James 3:6)."

Our Goal: To produce the maximum amount of life by speaking that which the Father is currently speaking within us, through our fellowship with the Spirit. (Jn. 14:10, 16).

Appendix B

Allowing God to Restore Your Visionary Capacity

Some find that vision is almost completely, or even totally, impossible. There may be several reasons why this is so. It is best to seek the Lord for revelation as to what the block or hindrance is, and then ask for His revelation as to steps to take to heal the problem. Following are some common problems which I have run into, along with some solutions which have proven helpful.

Problem #1 — Disdaining the visual and idolizing the rational

Some have unwittingly been swept into the westerner's idolization of logic, and disdain (or disregard) of the visionary. Westerners generally do not believe in the value and power of the visionary capacity within them. They do not hold it in esteem and honor, as one of the gifts which God has placed within man.

In healing this problem, one has to: 1) repent for not fully honoring and using a gift and capacity which God has placed within; 2) repent for idolizing logic and cognition; 3) state his commitment to honor and use his visual capacity as greatly as he honors and uses his analytical capacity; 4) ask God to breathe upon and restore his visual capacity; and 5) begin practicing and exercising it by learning to live in pictures as readily as he lives in thoughts. Then he is ready to begin presenting the eyes of his heart to God to fill **by looking** for His vision as he walks through life.

Problem #2 — Fear of entering into cultism

Some are unable to use their visual capacities effectively because they have been taught that it is cultish.

In healing this problem, one must: 1) realize that the ability to think and see using pictures was given to man by God, not by satan; 2) realize that even though satan seeks to fill man's visual capacity, so does God; 3) acknowledge that God does not want us to turn away from use of the visual capacity, but rather, He wants us to present it continuously to Him to fill; 4) renounce fear of receiving a satanic counterfeit, while confessing faith in God's ability to fill the visual capacity; 5) confess fear as sin, and receive God's gift of faith; 6) realize that satan can attack the thought processes as easily he can attack the visionary processes; therefore, both must be presented continuously before the Lord for Him to fill and to flow through.

Problem #3 — Cutting off the visual capacity in order to avoid the sin of lust

Some people have chosen to deal with the problem of lust by simply making a decision to cut off all use of the visual capacity. These people probably cannot visualize anything, including their living room couch.

In healing this problem, one has to: 1) realize that there are effective means of dealing with lust, other than cutting off one of the capacities which God has placed within; 2) learn to appropriate some of these other alternatives to effectively deal with the sin of lust; 3) repent for cutting off the visual capacity; 4) ask God to restore it and recreate it; 5) begin using it again; and 6) ask God to fill it with His divine vision.

Problem #4 —Cutting off the visual capacity in order to avoid some unpleasant visual scene

Some people have cut off their sensitivity to the visual capacity because they have been trying to avoid seeing a scene of pain in their lives. This may be a scene of molestation, or a recurring nightmare of snakes, or some other terrorizing scene. They have decided that the most effective way of handling these frightening scenes is to cut off their visual capacities.

In healing this problem, one has to: 1) recognize and discover the precipitating cause of cutting off his visual sense; 2) offer the scene to God; asking Him to walk into it and heal it with His loving, all-powerful presence; 3) ask God to restore the use of his visual capacity; 4) begin again using pictures and visions as he walks through life; and 5) present the eyes of his heart to God for Him to fill and flow through.

In summary, these are a few of the common blocks which keep people from living effectively in their God-given gift of dream, vision, and imagination. May each one learn to fully use all the capacities which God has provided within Man.

Appendix C:

Summary Diagram of Death of a Vision

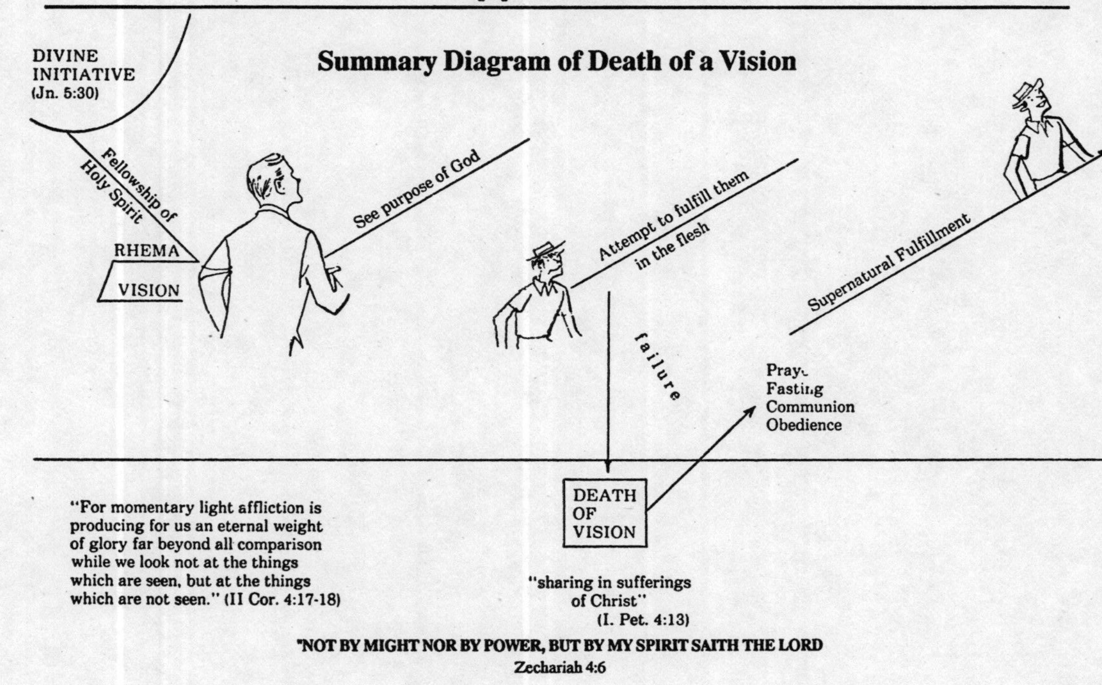

"For momentary light affliction is producing for us an eternal weight of glory far beyond all comparison while we look not at the things which are seen, but at the things which are not seen." (II Cor. 4:17-18)

"sharing in sufferings of Christ"
(I. Pet. 4:13)

"NOT BY MIGHT NOR BY POWER, BUT BY MY SPIRIT SAITH THE LORD

Zechariah 4:6

APPENDIX D:

Other Lessons Abraham Learned in His Walk of Faith

A. Partial Obedience To Full Immediate Obedience

Abraham's walk of faith began in Genesis 12:1-3, with the spoken word of God, revealing God's direction for his life and giving promises of a great nation that was to flow from his loins. He was 75 years old at the time. Abraham was not able to walk in total faith and obedience at this time; instead of "leaving relatives" as he was commanded, he took Lot with him (Genesis 12:4).

You will note that God required growth from his partial obedience to full obedience, separating Abraham from all his relatives, after which he began showing him the fulfillment of His promises (Gen. 13:14-18).

By the time Abraham was 99, he had learned the lesson of total obedience (Gen. 17). As God added the command of circumcision, Abraham obeyed "on the very same day as God had said to him (17:23)." This opened the way for God to commune immediately with Abraham again (18:1), whereas, his earlier disobedience brought long years with no communion.

We, too, must learn that simple total obedience moves the hand of God.

B. Doubt To Faith In God

In Genesis 12:10-20, we find that doubt and fear filled Abraham's heart. He feared that Egyptians would take his wife and kill him, thus doubting God's provision to keep him. Years later he still faced the same doubt (Gen. 20:1-18), lying again to help protect himself. However, Abraham did learn to have faith in God and when given a final test, that of offering Isaac on the altar, Abraham **believed** in the provision and strength of God.

He believed God would even raise him from the dead (Heb. 11:17).

We too must move from doubt to faith in God.

C. Unconditional Love — Gen. 13;14

In Genesis 13, Abraham offered to settle a dispute with his nephew by allowing Lot to choose first the area of land he desired. Lot choose the best, leaving the poorer to his uncle.

In Genesis 14, we find Lot in trouble and Abraham reaching out in love to save his nephew.

We too must learn to reach out in acts of love toward those who have hurt us.

D. Faithfulness to God — Gen. 14:17-24

Although the spoils of war rightfully belonged to Abraham, he refused to take them, preferring instead to keep an oath he had made to God (14:22-24).

We too must learn to set aside even rightful things in life in favor of keeping our word with God.

E. The Failure of Self-Effort — Gen. 16

While waiting for God to fulfill His promise, Abraham acted on the impatient suggestion of Sarah his wife (16:2). She suggested that he have children through her maid. This suggestion caused contention and controversy from then even until today as their descendants still war with each other. God would not accept their self-effort as a replacement for His supernatural provisions (17:19).

We must wait in patience before God, knowing that our self-effort only brings ruin.

F. Intercession for the Righteous — Gen. 18:20-33

Upon hearing of impending destruction upon Sodom and Gomorrah, Abraham begins interceding for the righteous ones, asking God to spare them. Thus, God's supernatural provision was brought forth and they were saved.

We too must learn to intercede on behalf of the righteous.

G. Summary — The Lessons to be Learned

1. Simple faith
2. Simple obedience
3. Unconditional love
4. Faithfulness to God
5. Overcoming self-effort
6. Interceding for the righteous

Communion With God — The Package of Materials

This is the most practical, down to earth teaching available in the world today training Christians how to dialogue with God. Over 99 percent of all participants begin to use vision in their prayer lives and write down pages and pages of dialogue with Almighty God on a regular basis. If you are not completely satisfied with this material and do not personally begin to receive and record the things the Lord is speaking to you, you may return this material in re-salable condition within 30 days for a **full money back refund.**

Communion With God Student's Workbook: a 150 page "write in" study manual. Mark Virkler teaches through this text on both the video and audio cassettes. $13.95

Communion With God Teacher's Guide: Twenty-two lesson outlines corresponding to the 22 video and audio sessions, laying the course out in detail for the leader/teacher. $11.95

Communion With God Video Tapes: 22 half-hour sessions of Mark Virkler teaching in a classroom setting. Purchase $299. Rental $99.

Communion With God Audio Cassettes: 22 half-hour sessions of Mark Virkler teaching through Communion With God. This corresponds exactly to the video series, except for an additional tape with four quieting exercises on it. $42.00

Dialogue With God: A 250 page teaching testimonial sharing not only the teaching of Communion With God, but also many pages of inspiring stories and testimonies. Included are 30 pages of journaling from individuals across several nations — a great source of encouragement for those beginning to journal. $6.95

Talking With Jesus: A 365 day devotional with Scripture and journaling for each day of the year. Evelyn Klumpenhouwer, the author, learned to hear God's voice in a Communion with God seminar in Canada in 1986. This book stands as a testimony of the power of the message of Communion With God, to actually teach people to hear God's voice. Tremendously life-giving. $7.95

Our Father Speaks Through Hebrews: A devotional of Hebrews by Rev. Peter Lord. Each journal entry has a verse from Hebrews followed by what the Lord spoke to Rev. Peter Lord concerning the truths in the verse. The first book of journaling produced by a man. Excellent, inspiring and life-giving. $7.95

Testimony

Dr. Richard Watson — Oral Roberts University

Communion With God by Mark and Patti Virkler has dramatically changed my prayer life. I have found I can will to dialogue with Christ on a daily basis, and I do. I believe this inspired approach to be absolutely essential to the growth of every serious Christian. I further believe **Communion With God** is an excellent example of the uniquely powerful way God is reaching out to His people today."

Rev. Thomas Reid — Full Gospel Tabernacle

"The course **Communion With God** is GOING TO CHANGE THE NATION by building a new generation of people that hear God's voice and dream God's dreams."

Spirit Born Creativity — The Package of Materials

The only book of its kind, teaching the process of releasing the creativity of God through the heart of the believer; This 238-page book is ideal for businessmen, parents and anyone who wants to become more creative. Textbook $8.95; Teacher's Guide available $4.95.

Counseled By God — The Package of Materials

A revolutionary book showing you plainly how you can find healing for the basic emotional needs of your life by dialoguing through them with God. It deals with such topics as healing anger, fear, inferiority, and condemnation, allowing Christ to heal deep hurts from the past, and learning to incubate only God's voice and vision. If you have found the deep healing that comes as this book has guided you into interaction with God, you may want to obtain other supporting materials for either your personal use or for group use.

Counseled by God Textbook a 130 page stand alone trade paperback. Excellent for personal use. $6.95

Counseled By God Student's Workbook: A 130 page "write in" study manual. Excellent for group use. Mark Virkler teaches through this text on both the video and audio cassettes. $8.95

Counseled by God Teacher's Guide: Twenty-two lesson outlines corresponding to the 22 video and audio sessions, laying the course out in detail for the leader/teacher. $8.95

Counseled by God Video Tapes: 11 hours of Mark Virkler teaching in a classroom setting. Purchase — $299, Rental $99.

Counseled by God Audio Cassettes: 11 hours of Mark Virkler teaching through **Counseled by God**. This corresponds to the video series. $42.00

Mark Virkler is Available as a Seminar Speaker

Mark travels full time conducting Communion With God and other seminars at churches worldwide. Contact him at 716-655-0647 concerning arrangements to have him come to your church.

Testimonies

Rev. Peter Lord — Park Avenue Baptist Church

"I have been an active Baptist pastor for thirty-seven years. As far as I am personally concerned, seminars like "Counseled by God" and "Communion With God," and "Abiding in Christ" are absolutely fundamental to the building up of the inner life. At this present time we have six ongoing classes in "Communion With God" using Mark's video series and one class on "Counseled by God." I highly recommend him and his ministry to you. I would be glad to talk with you on the telephone if you have any questions." 407-269-6702.

Rev. Judson Cornwall, ThD.

"God has especially graced Brother Mark Virkler to help persons re-discover the art of communion with God. I have had the opportunity to observe this from a distance for a number of years, but I now have joined forces with this brother in seeking to get this teaching to an ever wider segment of the body of Christ.

"I would highly recommend Mark Virkler and his seminar **Communion With God** to all who still desire to do the will of the Father. His approach is both unique and God given. His integrity is well documented, and his value in bringing people into a depth of prayer cannot be over estimated."

Communion With God Ministries

Name ______________________ Phone __________
Address __________ City __________ State ____ Zip ______

Qty	Title	Price	Total
	Communion With God		
______	Communion With God Student's Workbook	$13.95	______
______	Communion With God Teacher's Guide	$11.95	______
______	Communion With God Audio Cassettes	$42.00	______
______	Communion With God Video Tapes		
	______VHS ______Beta Purchase	$299.00	______
	______VHS ______Beta Rental	$99.00	______
______	Dialogue With God	$6.95	______
______	Talking With Jesus	$7.95	______
______	Our Father Speaks Through Hebrews	$7.95	______
	Counseled By God		
______	Counseled By God Paperback textbook	$6.95	______
______	Counseled By God Student's Workbook	$8.95	______
______	Counseled By God Teacher's Guide	$9.95	______
______	Counseled by God Audio Cassettes	$42.00	______
______	Counseled by God Video Tapes		
	______VHS ______Beta Purchase	$299.00	______
	______VHS ______Beta Rental	$99.00	______
	Cultivating Individual and Corporate Creativity		
______	Spirit Born Creativity textbook	$8.95	______
______	Spirit Born Creativity Teacher's Guide	$4.95	______
______	What the Bible Says About Silver and Gold	$3.95	______
______	Twenty Key Biblical Principles for Christian Management	$9.95	______

Shipping and Handling Charges

		Sub-total	______
U.S.	8%		
Canada	12%	Shipping & handling	
South America	16%	($2.50 minimum)	______
Europe, Africa, Asia, & Australia	20%	Total enclosed	______

Please allow 6-8 weeks for delivery to overseas countries. COD available in U.S. only

Money Back Guarantee: If you are not completely satisfied with these materials, you may return them within 30 days in re-salable condition, and receive the full refund on the cost of the book.

Make **check payable** in U.S. currency to: **Communion With God Publishers,** 1431 Bullis Road, Elma, NY 14059. 716-655-0647

______ A **free ordering catalog describing over 50 guided self discovery study manuals** (many with cassettes and videos) which Mark and Patti have developed. These are ideal for personal, small group and large group use, including home cell groups, Sunday school, Bible school, and Sunday and Wednesday evening church services. In addition to the above topics, this includes studies in the areas of abiding in Christ, Spirit born creativity, Christian dream interpretation, through the Bible series, creating and releasing wealth, worshipping with sign language, transmitting Spirit life, and much more.

______ A **free** copy of **"In Touch"**, a magazine which keeps you informed of new materials and developments in Mark And Patti's ministry, "Communion With God."

______ A **free** listing of 13 **seminars by Mark Virkler,** available to be hosted by your local church.